Be Human, Not a Zombie

A Guide to Finding Your Fundamental Nature

Pawel Wegrzyn

- May life continue
to reveal magic
for yours in every
place that you
seek.

With Love,
Paul Wehr   2023

Disclaimer: I do not want to implant beliefs or knowledge into your mind; don't take anything you read as the truth. The purpose of this writing is to open your mind enough for you to start experiencing the truth for yourself, as I experienced truth by looking within myself. What is offered here may be a different way of gaining knowledge, especially if you have spent your life gaining information from traditional sources outside of yourself. No matter how much knowledge you get from the outer, it will always be distorted, and not the ultimate truth; even our language is only a made up symbol of pure truth.

Contents

+

BRIEFING

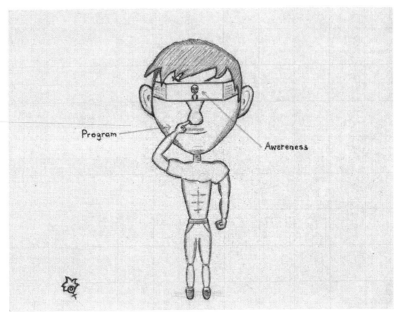

Programmed

My Experiment

Hypothesis:

That there is a practical way to tap into and live from my truest nature, as frequently as possible without being taken over by my programs (Zombie Mode).

Test Subject:

Me

The Problem:

Zombie Mode (Programmed, Ego-run, Unconscious)

The mode in which the majority of humanity operates—run by their mind without their conscious attention involved.

Techniques Used and Duration of My Experiment:

Meditation, yoga, empirical investigating, and self-mastery work (over 10,000 hrs.)

Who I Am Not

I am not a monk or a guru or any other
mythological being. I am as ordinary as one
comes. I grew up mostly in a Western manner; I
would hang out with my friends, play video
games, draw, and compete in sports. Mostly I
was the quiet type who observed things going on
and never said much, unless I really needed
too.

All my life I had so many questions about
what goes on inside me, and it felt like I
could never understand my controls, which kept
me living in my fantasies. I was pretty good at
most things I did, not usually because of
talent but because I was self-driven. My
biggest struggle in life has always been the
battle with me; my main competitor was always
me, and I could never understand why. Why did I
have so many stories, doubts, and fears—all
with myself? These things stopped me from
experiencing things just as they were:
experiences, rather than the stories and battle
I made them into in my mind.

I got really passionate about tennis and
attained a really high level of expertise,
eventually getting a tennis scholarship in the
US. The reason I am mentioning this is because
this is when I really started to see the full
effects of my mind on the experiences I was
having. I probably practiced more than most
people; I would train, hit against the wall,

serve, or do drills, and for some reason it was never enough. I did master skills, but not enough to silence my mind or even make it happy. It would always come in and take over, especially in tournaments. I tried everything: I listened to tapes, did breathing exercises, talked with people; I tried visualization techniques, and so on, but even with all that, I was still taken over by my uncontrollable negative thoughts and beliefs before the match started, and I continued to abuse by myself during and after the match.

Now that I look back, this was my chronic habit in most areas of my life—in school, in social gatherings, and anywhere else I was. I had many sad days. They seemed to outnumber happy ones, and I often wished that I was dead. But I didn't have the courage to do that because, even in that instance, my mind would come up with a thousand different scenarios of failure.

I grew up in a loving family, and my parents did all that they could to raise me and my siblings well. I even received a ton of attention, because tennis was my dad's passion as well.

Now that you know my back story a bit, you can have a clearer picture and see that I am no different than you. My life experiences might be different, but the opposition is the same in your life and the lives of others; simply, it's your mind. The reason that I am so certain of this is because I spent the last four years of my life trying to figure out what the hell is going on upstairs—mostly through meditation, yoga, an empirical investigation, and self-mastery.

I quit my career, as that wasn't bringing me anywhere closer to understanding why only some days I was kind of happy, and most other days I was just going with society's flow. I stopped working full time and began sitting under trees in parks and just observing what was going on inside me. I tried many techniques, but mostly I just sat and sat and investigated. Might sound boring, but it's amazing what you start unraveling when you stop gathering outside knowledge and go straight to the source within.

The main reason why this book has come into being is that I would like you to have the information that I received, and not just by reading this, but by experiencing this in your life. If you are interested in starting to understand life more fundamentally, and not just going by what society is doing, then this could be a guide to get you there. The book is not a magic pill; it's more of a seed that, if planted and cared for, could sprout a whole new understanding of who you really are and how to live life from that authentic place more often.

I am not trying to teach you anything beyond your understanding already. The problem is that we are all lazy, so, accepting that, basically I'm just trying to point you in the right direction. These insights that I have gathered are all experiential and not just read and parroted from a book. You can start experiencing all this, and what you learn for yourself. And you will need to if you want to understand something beyond what I am offering you from the outside.

Symptoms of the Human Race

Let's open your mind a little bit by talking about the state of consciousness in our world today. Hopefully this won't be a real shock to you, but you never know. If you are already able to separate from your mind at times, then you may be aware that the planet in its current state is occupied by mostly unconscious humans, and if you don't believe me, just observe the madness on our planet today yourself, or just observe your life in more detail and notice how your state of consciousness fluctuates.

If you take some time and observe our world from a bigger perspective than yourself, you will notice that the earth provides us with all the resources that we need to live well, yet we are not satisfied with this and have decided to take it upon ourselves to make things better. Here is the better that we have created:

We consume mostly artificial foods, yet real stuff grows everywhere. We brainwash our kids into believing what they should be consuming, achieving, and doing. We think that we are the most important species in the universe, as the things that we do to other beings perfectly exemplify this notion. We don't take the time to learn, yet we tell everyone else what is right or wrong. Last but not least, we think that the more things we can accumulate in the physical world, the happier we will be.

In short, we are run by the programs that we pick up through our development and, instead of taking the time to figure out how we function ourselves, we just blame others—like they know what the hell is going on.

How This Happens

Imagine you are a computer. In the beginning you come brand new, with just a couple of necessary programs downloaded into you. You are purchased, you go to your owner's home (parents) and get downloaded with more and more programs of their liking; some owners are very vigilant about the programs they put into you, and some just put in anything. You then start gaining more knowledge as the programs seem to help you understand things on this planet, but at the same time they take up space and need energy to run, and many times they intervene with other programs and are limited in many ways. Eventually there are so many programs downloaded into you that you don't even know which ones are there anymore, and furthermore, which ones are even useful. Your operating system (the Mind) is given control by you to run the programs and has the power to decide which ones it should run, and when, while you are not paying attention (in the Present Moment). Does this make sense?

This is how we operate in our day-to-day lives. You can see this in your own life just by observing yourself for five minutes and noticing that you barely ever reside in the present moment. Your attention is almost always occupied by the future and/or past. You live there fantasizing, while your programs that have been downloaded into you through your development have full control over the present moment.

The Problem

Zombie Mode

The reason for this experiment was to deal with this mode in which we reside for most of our lives. What is this Zombie Mode, you might be asking. Well, I have come to describe it as an unconscious, programmed, ego-driven state.

I called it Zombie Mode because it triggered an automatic response in me; I felt like I was doing things without any reason. It's as if a switch flicks and all of a sudden I became something else. Not really evil or always angry, but definitely disconnected and in some kind of trance state (asleep). Naming the state Zombie Mode also helped me to understand why, as a species, we have been able to do the awful things that we have done and continue to do—to ourselves, humanity, and the planet.

The Switch

How It Occurs

As your attention is taken into your mental activity (thoughts and emotions), your operating system switches to automatic programmed mode (Zombie Mode) and operates you in the present. If this didn't occur, then you would be dead pretty quick probably, as your awareness level of what is going on around you is very low when you are stuck in your head.

Some of these automatic programs are ones that you are born with and they are useful; others you download and implement through your development.

How to Know When You're Switching to Zombie Mode

Anytime you leave the present moment and get stuck in the mind, you are being taken over by Zombie Mode. You can notice this happening by how you feel; if you are anxious, worried, rushed, stressed, or basically not feeling at peace, then you have been taken over by your mind and are trapped in the thoughts and stories it plays for you while it operates you.

How to Get Out of Zombie Mode

At any moment you can notice yourself getting taken over, or perhaps you are already noticing that you have been taken over by Zombie Mode for some time; just the awareness of you being able to see it and accept it can switch you back to consciousness. You can also put your attention into your senses since those are always in your direct experience.

EXPLAINING THE CORE

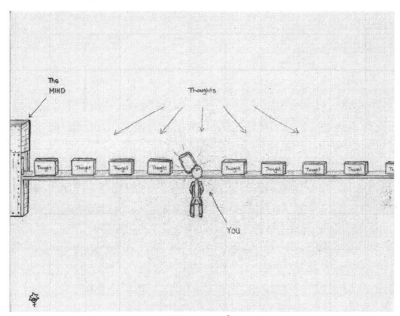

Trapped

The Mind

In order to get you more convinced about how the mind uses you—more than *you* use it—I will explain how it works, according to my observations. But first, I just want to be clear: I am not saying that the mind is evil or not useful. I am just saying that it has gotten way too powerful, and unfortunately has taken over humanity. The main purpose of our mind is to gather, analyze, calculate, and store information that may be useful to us when needed. Today though, if you take a closer look at our society, you will notice that our mind has become so powerful that we have become its little puppet, feeding it so much information that it then uses to create all types of fictitious stories that we get captured by, instead of living in the present moment, a.k.a. reality. Even your identity is mind created. All the things that you think that you are and perceive are derive from the mind.

Witness in your own experience that the things that you fear are a result of your mind repeatedly telling you that they are scary—by showing you (words and images), as well as linking to them body sensations (which you then associate to the emotion of fear)—all of which causes you to eventually accept as fact that certain things are scary. One common fear is spiders, but substitute any fear you like here. Let's examine why you and other people are afraid of spiders. It is not because they are really scary or evil; it's because every time you see a spider, your mind tells you all types of stories about it through thoughts and learned emotions, such as: thousands of spiders might crawl on you, into your nose, ears, mouth, as well as bite you, and whatever else you've accepted as true from the blockbuster film you long ago created and continually recreate. In this **example**, you have been captured by your mind's stories (words, images, and emotions) and are living in fiction and not in the actual reality that there is just one little spider in front of you in the current moment. Therefore, if you remain totally present in the moment and keep doing this each time you see a spider, rather than letting your mind take over, you will see that your fear will become less and less frequent, and eventually you might even enjoy spiders.

How the Mind Operates

Thoughts

This is one of the mind's tools that you are very familiar with, and not because you are an expert on how they work, but mostly because you have been consumed by them all your life. Thoughts seem to come in two forms, words and images, and they capture your attention with their content. This is how most people seem to perceive thoughts. But in this experiment, what we are most interested in are the sensations that occur when you have a thought. When you can expand your awareness enough, you can start noticing thoughts in this way and not the typical manner (stuck in their content)

Emotions

As I witnessed in myself, emotions seem to be a learned categorization of sensations (energy) that flow through us. These energetic sensations become linked to thoughts (Hebb's law: neurons that fire together wire together) and after repeated experiences, or even just one very powerful experience, emotions will accompany sensations and the experiences that evoke them, in order to provide a more powerful experience. Emotions are therefore created by or linked to the mind and they get you stuck in Zombie Mode.

Emotions can be triggered by events, people, memories, images, thoughts, and they can cause you to act in all sorts of ways, as the power they seem to bring with them almost seems unbearable at times. They have the ability to suck you in for long periods of time and when you are trapped inside them, the images and stories they bring are never ending.

Good **examples** of this are a death of a person, a break-up, a loss in a competition, a fight with a friend, etc. All these types of situations can bring you into extreme states of emotional and mental captivity (Zombie Mode).

The worst part in all of this is that you will even get sabotaged into believing that you should feel and think certain things or you are a bad person and have no feelings. If you experience periods of time where you are overwhelmed with emotions, just try to accept them, and go toward them, instead of trying to escape them. While you are doing this, notice that your thoughts have captured you and are keeping you stuck in past or future stories; accept that as well. Once you can notice this happening, you can start to try to get back into the present moment as frequently as possible to start diminishing the power of your mind over you. The key is acceptance; just being aware and accepting when emotions and thoughts take over you—not fighting or exaggerating them—just that awareness can help you break free from them.

Tip:

The less identified you become with mental activities (thoughts and emotions), the less suffering you will experience in life. You are not the mind.

Reality

An important "given" in this experiment is that every time you are not in the present moment, you are stepping out of REALITY, and you are surfing either in the FUTURE or the PAST. The worst part of this is that these imagined future and past illusions feel quite real, and it is sometimes hard for you to tell the difference.

The best way to begin to get clarity is to define reality for yourself as the present moment, because whatever you experience in the now is experienced by your senses and not your mind. As I mentioned before, the mind plays a lot of tricks, so let's not put our trust in the mind; we have done this for so many years and we can see where it has gotten us.

Another reason why we don't live in reality is because our mind is always about "bettering" our life. Yes, we have to admit that reality sometimes isn't ideal, but it is the real thing, and if you allow your mind to grab hold of you and time travel, to the past or future, then you are just escaping reality briefly. I have spent many moments in my life being caught in both, the past and future, and I can tell you that although it might make you feel better on the level of the mind, it is not doing anything but postponing what is real.

Many people get stuck in mind-created fiction, because it's not always so easy to face the fire, but it's only a fire because your mind interprets it as one. If you actually go toward whatever is real, it is never as bad as your mind has made it to be, unless after the fact, your mind again captures you and plays recaps of what just happened and why it was horrible. If you primarily live in the present moment, then all you will be facing is reality, and I don't know about you, but facing something real seems like common sense to me.

Awareness

Awareness is seeing the world as it is without your or society's inputs. When we are brought into this life, we come equipped with this ability to be aware of everything. But it takes time for a human to develop all necessary capabilities to function on the physical world, and we eventually forget how to use this primal skill or even know that it is useful. The more we learn, the more we get consumed by our own knowledge, and we start believing that this is the ultimate way of knowing.

Awareness grows every time you just can observe the world without adding to it, and just accept how it is. Most people get taught by society and then tricked by their mind that learned intellectual knowledge is most important. They then can't ever let anything be without trying to know it intellectually—your mind comes in and keeps you quite busy. It also prevents you from connecting to that object fully and outside of that knowledge. When a person is able to use their full sensory capabilities to witness life, instead of just using the mind, amazing things start happening. You store the information with a different knowing, a knowing that uses the whole body to experience the event, not just a knowing that is conceptualized and stored in the mind.

Think of awareness as the total knowing of the universe. The more your awareness expands, the closer you are to the ultimate truth of YOU. Right now your awareness of who you are is very small, or low-level, because probably you haven't been doing this work. You may think you are your body, or mind, or whatever else you believe. However, if you investigate the nature of a belief, you will find that it is just a deeply engrained thought that you have assumed is true—as others have done as well.

The more often you separate from the mind, the more you can absorb through observation. Contemplate the possibility that when you think you know everything, you stop allowing awareness to reveal truth for you.

Consider this **example:** When you think that you know a bird, your mind will tell you the name, colors, size, ability, shape, etc. All these things are aspects you added to that piece of life that, in fact, exists independent of your qualifications. And by adding these qualifications, automatically your ego will use the knowledge or lack of it as a determining factor in your intelligence and how much you know compared to others. You then get blinded, believing you know this thing and you can't ever see it any other way—especially for what it truly is. You don't really see it; you just know it, and in a very limited way. Like the bird, we are multidimensional, and seeing something just with the eyes and maybe ears is just a partial knowing. We are looking for the

most fundamental knowing of existence, and that
is outside of any conceptualizations we have
added on top of the items we describe.

Truth

To take this experiment on, you have to understand that we are in this mess because we believe things blindly. Knowing truth is not a popular endeavor for most people in this world; you can probably tell that we live in a very low-conscious society, where the majority of our information is a bunch of lies. Just look at the food industry or advertisements in general; most of them are hiding and manipulating information in order to achieve something—sell you something. Here, we are concerned with the truth of YOU. This is the main issue. It is not a competition game. Instead of spending all our time complaining that the world is run terribly and is corrupt, we need to start noticing that we—our fake selves—are the ones who help create it that way, and we need to unmask our Truth.

The whole problem is our beliefs: we take in information throughout our lives, especially in our development, without making sure that the information that we are taking in is truthful to the ultimate degree. Yes, of course there are many years when you don't have the capacity to even question anything, but nobody stops you from doing it later on.

Why aren't more people thinking about this and how important it might be to try to investigate what you are at your most fundamental truth? The answer is complex in nature, but ultimately it is that we are distracted with all the other stuff that goes on, and we don't value truth enough to take this upon ourselves.

Have you ever taken the time to notice that even our language is made up? We created it by placing names and symbols on top of reality and then we've assumed that it is what we called it: man, woman, bird, tree. We teach this language to others, as it is useful to communicate, but eventually, over years and centuries, we start believing that the name and symbol are that object. A tree isn't really a tree if you look at it in the most fundamental way; it is something that can't be described, as the description is us overlaying something on top of it.

The same goes with you: you were given a name and told many things that you are, and things that you are not, and then you just started believing that you are your name and body, and whatever else you believe. The more beliefs, the more problems occur, and the more limited your experience of life is, and your connection to your true nature.

The beauty with humans is that we have the ability to do wonderful things with our large brains, but unfortunately we haven't noticed that, as we've learned and used the brain in more complex ways, we have gotten further away from truth.

EXPLAINING THE EXPERIMENT

Up to U

Dis-identifying

To start understanding what your truest nature
is, you first have to start removing
unnecessary clutter that you have gathered over
the course of your life. What is clutter? It is
everything that isn't you. To find what is not
you, you must probe deeply—not a very common
practice around the world. Most people live
life as if they are their body, mind, and maybe
some spiritual aspect as well. On top of that,
they believe that they are separate from other
people and other beings. Then on top of that,
they think that they are their name, race,
nationality, beliefs, ideologies, etc.

I can separate these belief items into
even more categories, but the point is for you
to start finding and observing what you really
are, and not subcategorize all the descriptors
you have gathered and understand each of them
separately. All you really need to know is that
there are many things you are not, and you've
gathered them all—into a massive heap of
clutter.

Most people are too caught up in "normal"
life to even start an investigation of this
kind, and if they contemplate investigating,
they are confused about how to even approach
it.

Lucky for you, my primary purpose in this
book is to give you tips and a push, hopefully
to start you in this experiment. Merely reading

this information about an unknown investigation means little if you don't experience it. What I'm talking about is something new that cannot be learned by words or through the mind, as it is beyond that way of knowing.

So how do you begin?

Questioning

In order to start your investigation, you have to get out of your mind, and you can do this by asking it questions that it cannot answer logically. It will try to answer them, but it will not produce concrete answers, and thus, it will create an opening—a vacuum—for real truth to fill.

The main questions that I use when I am trying to separate from my mind's hold on me are as follows:

WHO AM I? WHAT AM I?

WHERE DO I EXIST?

WHAT IS EXISTING?

WHAT AM I OUTSIDE OF MY NAME AND ALL THINGS I HAVE GATHERED?

IS THIS REAL?

WHAT IS REALITY?

The point of these questions is not for your mind to come up with answers. We are not interested in that. The point is for you to start experiencing what goes on when your mind is not in control. Your attention can now be on the sensations that occur inside and outside of your body; this is what you are looking for.

It is really important to be able to start being aware of the difference between your mind's thoughts and your body's sensations when your mind has your full attention, and when you can separate from it and shift the attention to other areas. Awareness is a skill that you can grow, so don't get discouraged when you get captured in your thoughts; this will happen constantly. This is the battle we are trying to overcome.

Observing

Get used to this one, because this will be your new way of investigating and learning. It may sound easy, but it's quite complicated to just observe, as the mind will not allow you to do this in silence. You need to be aware anytime the mind tries to grab your attention and capture you in its stories (thoughts and emotions). So, BE WARNED! It is crucial that you understand that you will fall victim to the mind's trickery time and time again. The key is to not get discouraged and give up because, believe me, this will get frustrating. At times you will not even know you have been captured by your mind until a couple of hours into the distraction. It's quite remarkable how this is even possible, but this is why you're doing this work. The more you do it, the better and quicker you will find yourself identifying when you get deflected (or switched to Zombie Mode).

When observing, one way to not get captured by your mind is to put your attention into your senses, and keep it there as long as you can. Really be aware, especially of the sounds, the sights, and touch. By touch I mean all the sensations and pressure you feel throughout your body or when touching physical objects. For **example**, how your feet feel pressing on the floor, or the temperature in the room, or the sensations floating around inside you. Again, it is really important to not get caught up in trying to logically understand what you are hearing, seeing, or feeling; just keep observing all that is without judgements. The minute you have a judgment or thought about something you are observing, your mind has captured your attention and it will feed you all types of stories, analytics, and so on.

Tip:

Watch yourself from a distance without attachment to any one thing.

Benefits of this Experiment

As a normal, rational human being, you are probably wondering why this experiment is important in your life. Well, just from reading this far, you may have sensed some potential benefits, but I will briefly talk about the unbelievable transformation that this could lead to—if you are serious enough to undertake this journey. If you spend only a couple minutes investigating and then continue to live the exact same way that you are currently living, chances are that not much will change. But consider this: everything takes some effort, so you might as well be putting effort into self-mastery, rather than self-sabotage.

The majority of humanity, including you, suffers primarily from self-made problems, and the magnitude of these self-creations is far more than you might suspect. (As you read that sentence, perhaps your ego stepped in and got defensive. Take a breath, feel what that feels like, and be aware of this happening, as it/your ego does not like to hear what I am telling you.) Now try to be brutally honest—you don't have to tell anybody but yourself: Can you admit that your suffering occurs mostly in your head? Things such as stress, anxiety, worry, depression, pain, worthiness, self-esteem, self-love, anger, frustration, confidence, and basically any other issue that you think you may be suffering about is primarily caused because you think you are something that you are not and you believe it. Yes, some things like physical disabilities, mental disabilities, and actual physical pain are not as easy to dissolve, but even those can be diminished when you dis-identify with what you are not.

To dis-identify with these aspects, you have to really understand that your struggles are with you and not with the world. Ultimately the problem is that your mind does not let you act in ways that you wish it did act—and then your full potential is not reached. Try to really remember this, because I can guarantee that there have been multiple times in your life that you did not act in your most authentic manner because you were afraid to do so, as the consequences your mind conjured up at the time seemed way too great. This is the primary reason I have been on this search—because all my life, I felt like I have been limited and have not been able to live at my highest potential, due to all kinds of tactics created by my mind.

You are meant to be different and unique, and this is the beauty about you. The problem is that your mind makes you believe that this is not the right way to be, and society will not accept you if you embody your unique self. You can ignore this path to your unique self; you can dedicate yourself to being a zombie or robot, but I warn you strongly, that this will lead to tons of suffering, and confusion, as you are then always going against the current, and not with it. When you live from truth and authenticity, it doesn't take as much effort as living from lies, as lies require a mastermind to continue to conjure up and keep track of all the illusions and deceptions.

Imagine living in constant peace, joy, and love. Being connected to something way beyond your understanding. Imagine that your presence evokes similar states in others—no matter what is going on around you. This is the great benefit of this experiment.

Fundamental Nature

Now that you are a bit more aware of what is going on in the mind and in this world and I have maybe convinced you to embark on this experiment, it will be useful for you to understand your most fundamental nature, outside of your fictitious mind-created self.

After investigating this for thousands of hours, and finally touching this truth for myself, I can tell you that at your core you are an infinite being, fully connected to Source, God, or whatever other name you have given this Infinity. You can even go further with this and realize that you *are* this Source, but for some people this might be bothersome, as they pedestalize this entity. By being God (replace with your believed Source name), I don't mean you are better than others or more powerful, because if you accept this notion, you must also accept that others are God/Source also, as they are the exact same thing as you, living in their form. This can also be said of other beings, creatures, and life forms; they embody Source, and it is as much them, as it is you.

I used to struggle with this a lot, as I thought I was a shy, artistic tennis player, who wasn't worthy or empowered in most aspects of life. Then eventually I realized that all those things were not me and, better yet, they could not be me. How could gathered beliefs be you? It doesn't make sense, since you picked them up as you developed. Even your name is not you; it is just a fictitious appellation given to you.

When you start investigating and touching this Infinity that is you in actual experience, you will feel the utmost peace, joy, and love and even if the worst possible situations happen to you on the physical world, you can still feel this Infinity and live through it and realize that the situation that you are dealing with is just an experience and that is all—nothing more, nothing less.

This feeling of peace, joy, and love is not really understood until you experience it—outside of your mind. That is the whole experiment: we are trying to grow your awareness enough to be able to start experiencing this peace, joy, and love as often as possible. Through this experience of transforming our awareness, we will prove the hypothesis that there really is a practical way to tap into and live from your truest nature, as frequently as possible, without being taken over by your programs (Zombie Mode). And this way and awareness and subsequent experience of your true nature exist for you and others always.

I hope you can see how powerful this realization is. Once you are one with your true nature, you become one with what you really are. Your ego no longer runs your life and, thus, all the problems you think that you have are not the main focus of your life. You don't need to build up your ego by being better than others anymore, because you know that you are infinite, and so are they.

You become God. You start living from your most authentic nature and start seeing others in that same way. You then start living out your life's purpose, and that is anything that you love to do. And your overwhelming motivation for doing anything becomes to raise consciousness or to be of service to the world.

Tip:

This is beyond the mind and must be directly experienced. Strip away all that is not you to become It.

TECHNIQUES USED

Spying on self

Introduction

Now that you know the fundamental reasons why this experiment might be useful in your life, I will talk about how you can start and implement this in your life. Or at least I will offer what I have been doing. Just a warning: I took this to the extreme, as I wanted to learn this as quickly as possible—in all honesty, in order to help myself, but also to spread it to others.

I have used the techniques in the following chapters to pursue this experiment. Just remember that I, too, was a beginner in these techniques at one point, and I had no idea what I was doing or if I was doing it right. The mind will always come up with objections and provide you with enough mental dialogue to fill books, but we are not interested in the master mind here—so don't believe all the excuses it tells you. I will talk about each technique briefly so you are aware of what it is and why it will be useful.

Disclaimer: I am not in normal terms an expert in the field of any of these techniques. I definitely have spent enough time in all of these fields to get certifications or degrees, but I am not concerned with accruing credentials. I am just one human being who has had experiences that I am now using to guide you to start your own experiment. If you desire credentials, there are plenty of teachers who come with them. Or you can accrue your own by studying and learning the material presented here intellectually. But I guarantee you that no matter how much information you read or how many certifications you receive, it will only be knowledge and not experience if you don't make yourself the experiment and commit to being uncomfortable doing it.

Meditation

"But Meditation is boring," you might be saying, and "I can't sit for more than five minutes without things hurting and my mind driving me nuts." Well, there is your proof that you are run by your mind. Your mind is telling you these things, and you listen to it. You are taking orders. Everybody is. And most people are so scared of what the mind says, that they even think they could die if they don't eat something for twenty-four hours.

I am not saying this will be an easy process, but if you can tough out a couple sessions, you will find that meditation is one of the most powerful things in your life. When you are new to this, your mind is very powerful, dictating your life. But once you learn that most of the things it tells you are big fat lies, then you will start to enjoy meditating—as it is the process to observe this madness in real time—and it will become something you look forward to.

Now let's talk about what meditation is. I have come to realize that meditation is the ability to observe yourself without judgements, attachments, or any other mind-created stories. Meditation is the accepting of what is in reality at the current moment, without trying to control or alter anything.

The reason to add meditation to this experiment is that it offers a way for you to learn and invite intelligence to come in. When you separate from your mind and allow things to enter by making space, then realizations start popping up, and you just start understanding things; it's quite remarkable and super powerful.

My Meditation Experience

I dabbled in this practice for many years, as I always was trying to learn how to deal with my mind. As I mentioned earlier, I played high-level tennis and my mind would consume me and be my main downfall in competitions. For the first couple of years of meditation, my practices were infrequent and random. But around four years ago, I made meditation a daily practice, and some days I did it up to four hours—not in a row but interspersed throughout the day. I tried many different techniques, and I still mix the mode of meditation up at times, but mainly I just sit and observe.

Yoga

"That's girly, and I'm a man. I can't do that!" AHHH, so your still captured by your mind and societal thinking. Good luck with that; it seems to be going great for you. Again, notice all the baggage you carry on every subject. Have you even taken a look at what yoga is fundamentally, outside of your mind's and society's notions? Let's have a look.

You have a body, right? And you use it each and every day to do things, right? Do you know how it works? Nope! Probably not, since all you do to take care of it is probably feed it junk and maybe work out a bit. Right, work out! Why are you working out? "Because I want to look good and get strong." Oh, that makes sense. If society thought that skinny, muscleless humans were sexy, would you still work out? (BTW, I am not saying working out isn't good; I'm just asking you to observe your motivation for doing it.)

If you are stuck on what everyone is doing, and what's acceptable and what isn't, then you probably haven't figured out that you and the universe are linked, and that just by taking the time to learn your body and work on certain movements, it allows for intelligence to shine through it much easier. We download information no matter what. So you can choose to download what current society says, or you can learn from ancient wisdom to adjust yourself in certain proven ways that open new channels which directly connect you with source.

Yoga means union—being one with everything. Um, I don't know about you, but I'm down with being one with everything.

The reason we are implementing yoga in this experiment is that it will allow our bodies to receive information a lot more easily, since we are tuning in to the universal frequencies which you are definitely not aware of, nor can you likely feel. All matter is energy. And so are you. At your core, you are energy, and you are constantly vibrating. When you use your body, day in and day out, it starts having blocks and does not allow the energies to move through you as easily as they can if they are free. Today's yoga has become mainstream, and most of it is all show. But fundamentally it is a way to experience free energy flow by connecting deeper within the body. All you really need to do is use yoga to learn about yourself; you don't need to be become an acrobat. Try it. Find a class. If you start enjoying it and how you feel afterwards, you might want to continue practicing.

My Yoga Experience

I have been doing yoga for about six years now pretty frequently. As with meditation, the first two years, I wasn't so serious and I just did it because it felt good for my body. The last four years, however, I have been totally focused in learning my inner state. I took some group classes at first to learn the technique, but then quickly progressed on my own, since I am self-motivated. Just doing yoga alone can get you to understand your fundamental self, since yoga was created to do this. So by all means, add this practice to your life, but to progress quickly here, you must get out of mainstream yoga and learn it at its core.

Disclaimer: As mentioned earlier, I am not a credentialed practitioner. Advanced yoga practices can evoke a level of energy surge (Kundalini) that is best experienced with a qualified teacher. If, in your practice, you experience an energy that feels uncomfortable or in any way scary, consult a qualified teacher before continuing this practice.

Empirical Investigation

Maybe you've never heard of this word before. When I started this journey, "empirical" is what I became.

Basically, empirical means "looking within." Unfortunately average human beings gather information by looking outside themselves. I am by no means saying you can't learn things this way, but if you start looking inside, you will quickly notice that all the information gathered from outside is conceptualized, distorted, and limited.

As mentioned earlier, language is made up by us. Names that are given to things and nature are not really what they are, right? Names and language are merely a means to be able to communicate, and yes, this is beneficial on the level of the physical, but at the same time you must notice that words are not the things they describe; they are not the truth of anything. If you only live on the level of the language and the physical descriptions it offers, you will always know things on that level, and not beyond. This is great, but you are not just a physical being, so it might be a good idea to start learning other aspects of you as well—actually, more fundamental aspects of yourself and the universe.

The reason we are implementing this empirical way of learning is because we are not so concerned anymore about outer learning; you already know how to do that. We are trying to allow the truth to come in through us, and this is the way to do it. It is not forced or controlled. You must just become the empty space that allows truth to fill it. When you start learning to separate from the mind, you are creating an opening that is needed for this way of understanding to shine in.

My Empirical Investigating Experience

I guess you could say this practice was a natural thing for me, as I have always been questioning myself, but there was never any structure and real results until I coupled this questioning with meditating four years ago. When you start questioning and just observing, you find a lot of answers. You are not "thinking" them up; they begin to come to you as insights. They come at random times, so you really need to pay attention, because anything can trigger this. They can come after a week or months. Suddenly you get this aha moment, like OMG, I knew this but only now it is clear.

Self-Mastery

The more aware you become of what your true
nature is, the more you will be able to
disassociate yourself with the fake you and
start mastering your life on the physical
world. Right now you are holding yourself back
because your mind is playing all types of games
with you. It wants you to fit in, it wants you
to be normal, it wants to succeed, it wants to
be good, etc. Over your lifetime, you have been
trying to be so many things that you have had a
really tough time just being you.

Once you start letting go of your mind-
made self (ego), you will have the opportunity
to develop in any areas that you want. If you
really think about it, ultimately a person's
goal in life is to become their ultimate
version, and once you can start removing the
fakeness of you, you then can start working on
becoming that ultimate version. This takes an
effort, but once you are on this journey, you
will not want to live any other way.

We are given this amazing futuristic
body. Why use it with such limited potential?
We limit our potential not because we want to,
but because we get in our own way more than we
help ourselves.

The reason we are focusing on this area
of self-mastery in our experiment is because
once we get out of the illusion of what we are
not, we need to start implementing and living

through what we are. This will basically be your journey for life. You were kind of doing this already but very superficially and not with substantial results, as all the progress was ego driven, and not for your life purpose.

My Self-Mastery Experience

For most of my life I had no idea that I could really master myself. Obviously I would try to learn new skills, but I never really knew how to work on becoming a better version of myself— especially since I had my mind to deal with. Once I started the other practices (meditation, yoga, empirical investigation) seriously, self-mastery started coming naturally. This is my main goal in life right now and will be forever, as I now find it weird to just sit and allow my mind to keep me stagnant and prevent me from operating at my highest potential. Basically I carry this with me everywhere I go, and I am now aware enough that I can witness when I am not at my full potential and, thus, I reflect on it after it happens and I try to be aware if I continue to do this again. Most people, I've noticed, just accept that their mind holds them back in many aspects of their life; or they aren't even aware and they just live with the mind dictating everything. But the beauty of this work is that you don't have to live with it (the Zombie mind), and you can actually choose what is important to you and learn it.

Challenges of Beginning this Experiment

Okay, so for those of you who are still reading because you are interested in starting this experiment, I have an important message: it is important to not rush and think that—*poof*—magic will just happen super-fast and it won't take much effort. Living out this experiment will take quite a bit of effort, especially at first, as your mind will not like this. What I am urging you to do is not really mainstream stuff. People practice yoga for years without ever experiencing what I am asking you to do. People attend self-improvement workshops and never even approach the uncomfortable place where they are no longer who they thought they were—the experience that I am suggesting you explore. If you seriously commit to this experiment, you will be in the minority; you will not be able to talk about what you feel with most people. So, if you take this on, you will have to become committed yourself. There are going to be many challenges. Here are some of the main things that I've encountered when doing this.

Discouragement

Getting discouraged is probably one of the biggest battles that you will face, and this is going to happen quite often. Discouragement is your mind trying to distract you. You can believe its lies and excuses and let it tell you to stop practicing, or you can use this as a sign, and be like, "Oh, my mind doesn't want me to do this; let me keep going anyway. This is definitely not going to hurt me, so let me try to transcend my mind, even though it's telling me this practice isn't doing anything for me."

The problem is that we have been conditioned to believe so many things that our mind tells us. This happens with eating, with watching TV, with activities, etc. The key is for you to work despite discouragement. Start separating yourself from your mind and then make decisions without impulse, without being pushed around.

If you don't believe the mind is pushing you around, here is an **example:** We all know McDonalds meals are terrible for us. You eat them and afterwards you feel like garbage, yet the mind still tells you, "I want McDonalds!" Does it really though? This is what we are trying to do here—question rather than blindly believe. Spoiler alert: After investigating myself, the answer is, No I don't want to be poisoned. You are just doing it—eating McDonalds—out of a program that derives from advertising and popular culture.

Even if you are not currently questioning yourself on simple desires and beliefs, I'm asking you to believe me on this for now. Eventually you will gain enough willpower to do this for periods of time that are long enough that you start seeing results—new clarity, new insights. And the discouragement is only the mind's attempt at a roadblock.

People

The next challenge is people. As I said above, this is not mainstream stuff we are attempting, which means that your wife or husband, friends, family members, coworkers, and all other people who you come in contact with are all mostly still consumed by their minds, and they are living their lives in very unconscious ways. You are as well, but at least you already recognized this at some level and are trying to change. The challenge will be that when you aren't fully aware yet of what is going on, you will be getting consumed by other people's unconscious behavior without even noticing. This is how tricky this is: at one moment you are feeling fully conscious and aware of things, and then the next second you switch to Zombie Mode, because your mind has taken over. The mind is all about gaining its power through judging, competition, and comparing itself with others—which means, when you encounter people, your mind will be doing this automatically, and you will be sucked into this mental process.

Here is an experiment you can try: Go to the mall and observe people for a couple minutes, and really notice all the things your mind tells you about those people. This will especially happen with people you don't like for some reason—such as a race you have a history with, or the way a person looks or dresses, and according to any beliefs you currently hold about others. All these components of the mind will be in the forefront. But instead of you being aware of them, you will be stuck in the story they're creating.

As you work on meditation, you will start becoming the awareness that knows these components, and your awareness will actually start dissolving all these judgments and stories, as they are not the truth of those people. The funny part is that you don't even know those individuals, yet you dislike them because of all those beliefs your mind stores for you that you picked up from an experience or your family or TV or a magazine or school or wherever else you have been imprinted.

Success

Another challenge in doing this work is success. Our culture makes it seem like success is only measured in how much money you have, the level of schooling you've achieved, or the possessions you own. Yes, of course all these things have some benefit, as this is how our society runs, but you choosing to slave at a job for many more hours than you need to, in order to pay for your massive house, car, and all the other gadgets that you decided to have, is not necessary. There is nothing wrong with working long hours, but there is something wrong if we work long hours because we think happiness happens out there, and not from within.

For many people success is not being alone. They are uncomfortable being alone. And even when they are alone, they are on the phone or watching TV or having to do something because, again, their mind bullies them, and they have to keep busy to ward off thinking—to numb themselves.

Perhaps your ego is getting defensive: "But I have to work long hours just to survive and I have nothing." You can believe that if you want, but chances are that you have enough to live and you're just comparing yourself to others— as mentioned before, a great tactic used by the mind. Or "I have to stay busy because there are so many things I must do, and what if I miss something and get left behind? Alone!" Why not try being alone? Maybe you'll start to hear what nonsense your mind is spewing.

No, the success we are programmed to achieve is definitely not measured by how much you have mastered yourself.

Distractions

As our society is all about physical gains and filling our minds with as many activities as we can. We have created the ultimate wonderland, a place full of distractions. Our world has so many things that you can get sucked into that it is almost impossible to get out. From sports, to food, to clothes, to drugs, to entertainment in general, we are addicted to distractions. We can't live without them, and unfortunately these are all very low-conscious things. They don't have to be, but our society is run by unconscious people, and therefore we have created many unconscious things. I am by no means saying that you have to get rid of all these things and not participate in them anymore. I just want to open your mind enough to see that they are all distractions. You will see this for yourself if you take this experiment on, but for now, think as you wish and even defend your ego if you like.

Events

We humans are a busy species and we are constantly doing something or things are happening in our lives, sometimes good, sometimes bad. Events are going to come up and they will probably detour you from continuing this practice. There might be death, pain, struggles, sickness, break-ups, vacations, trips, competitions, marriages, children, etc.

All these things will challenge you and unfortunately probably win the battle against you continuing this practice. And yet, if you just realized that this practice—this experiment—provides the greatest tool for these types of moments, you might continue. Continue the experiment because it lets you become aware of events as a conscious being and not a zombie.

OWN PRACTICE

One

How to Start Your Own Practice at Home

Remember you do not have to start with anything too crazy; if you do, chances are you won't continue. What I would recommend is to implement this into your life in the following way:

Meditation

Start learning to meditate: **five minutes a day** is sufficient in the beginning (Set your long term aim to get to 30 min a day)

Pick a time to do this during your day—it doesn't matter when, just as long as you can be alone without distractions.

Set your phone to a five-minute timer and sit and observe things. (Do not check your phone until it beeps; notice that your mind will try to make you check, but resist.)

The following things will occur:

You will be uncomfortable, you will be asking yourself if you are doing it right, you will be annoyed with something, sucked into a thought, bored, in pain, thinking you are doing it wrong, and many other mind distractions. This is all normal, and even though all this is happening, don't give up! Last the five minutes even if it is absolutely dreadful. Allow anything to be in your present moment. If you feel sad, feel the sensations of it, without listening to your mind; just observe it.

Give yourself a month at least of this and then really reflect on what you learned from it. Then continue and maybe add some more time, especially on days you are struggling. It will be tough to do that, but if you do, you will learn a lot.

Tips:

1. When you sit, it doesn't matter how. At the beginning, just sit comfortably and try not to fall asleep.

2. Try to put your attention on all the sensations in your body, and try to keep it there as long as you can. Really zero in on the sensations and go toward them. Even if it doesn't feel that good, just accept the sensations anyway.

3. Really focus on the now—every single second, the now. If you leave the now and find yourself in a thought, try to come back to the present. Don't fight the thought; accept it and then again focus on your sensations.

4. Some days' meditations will feel better than others and you will feel like you're getting somewhere, and other days you will struggle and feel like you are going backwards. Accept that and notice that you can't control the day; just observe how it is.

5. Do not rush; just accept the five minutes.

6. Try to always separate yourself as much as you can from your current situation in life. Let go of everything, because your mind will try to play you problems and upcoming events constantly. Accept if it is trying to do this, and accept any thoughts that come in. Witness them, but then let them go instead of continuing to pay attention to them. Switch your focus back to the now and your senses.

7. Become the watcher of all that is at the current moment and try to not get attached to any one thing. Once you get attached to something and you realize this, watch again.

8. Observe the breath.

Journaling

As you start your meditation habit, it is crucial that you start journaling your experiences. This will be a way to really notice your programs and the way you have behaved after the fact. At the end of your practice or the end of the day, make it a priority to write down what you experienced throughout your sitting and throughout your day.

Key things to track if you are looking for structure:

1. Write down if you meditated and how it went today.

2. Your mindset during your day—were you feeling sad, happy, unworthy, lack, confident, etc. and write down what triggered the feelings or describe the situation they arose in.

3. Write down anytime you noticed yourself being stuck in thoughts, future or past, and whether or not you spent most of your time living in the present moment.

4. Write down how you experienced this day. Did you enjoy it or, if you didn't, what would you prefer to do differently or what behavior would you like to reprogram?

5. Write down what you are grateful for in your life; it could be even for having socks or shoes; there is always something.

6. Write down the things you want to start experiencing in your life and how you want to start becoming your best version of yourself. Do you want to eat better, be more conscious with what you spend your time on, and other things of this nature?

Empirical Investigation

Once you've been journaling and are consistently meditating for at least five minutes a day for a month, add the empirical investigation part to your meditation.

Do the exact same things as you would while you're meditating, and once you've connected to the present moment through your senses, start asking yourself some deep questions. I gave you a list of these in the questioning section **pp32**.

Ask a question and just sit and observe what happens when you ask that question. Don't try to answer it mentally; just notice what goes on and how the mind will try to answer it for you; be aware of all that is happening and ask again and continue doing this for the allotted time. You're not trying to understand anything here; you are just trying to observe what goes on when you question the mind. Continue watching from a distance so that you do not get sucked back into thoughts and believing what the mind tells you. If an answer to your question arises, question that answer with another question: such as, is this true?

The next week ask a different question and observe what happens and keep doing this.

The point is to continue to do this on a regular basis, so that you can start dis-identifying with all the things that you think you know and all the things that you think you are. We are not looking for what you think you know or what society has conditioned us to believe. We are just trying to touch the real truth outside of all those things. Basically we are trying to shake your wall of beliefs, so that it becomes loose enough to create an opening that allows us to reach the core.

You have to keep doing this deep questioning over and over to get to your most fundamental nature. You will feel at peace when you start touching this area. You will start connecting more to oneness, which is being connected with everything. You will start being truth.

Eventually though the mind will close the gap that was opened and you will have to start questioning once again. This will be a process, but once you poke enough holes in the mind made structure of lies; beliefs, ideologies, theories that are held by you currently, truth will start shining in from all openings and deception will be seen much more easily.

Yoga

Once you make a habit of these three practices, add yoga—if you aren't doing it already. Yoga is going to transform you, because it works with the body, and the body is much easier to deal with than your mind. You don't have to be an expert. Practicing a fifteen-minute routine with some fundamental yoga postures is adequate. As in meditation, as you practice yoga, observe all the sensations inside you, instead of getting sucked into thoughts. Basically meditate while you do yoga.

This will be a huge challenge and many times you will fail, but continue to practice again. And again. What most people do in mainstream yoga is seek amazing moments and become acrobats. What you need to do is accept every moment and witness what goes on inside you, instead of trying to feel good or just becoming the most flexible you can be; that will come as a by-product of this practice anyway.

Tip:

Focus on working with the breath as you do the postures. Allow the breath to flow through the body and back out. Learn to breathe deeply and to all areas of the body. The breath is a happening and just by observing it huge breakthroughs can occur.

Practice in Everyday Life

Now that you've added these routines to your life, you need to bring meditation into your daily life—beyond the five minutes a day. Instead of living like a crazy zombie during the rest of your day, start observing yourself going through life. Practice not getting sucked into and stuck in your mind.

You can use any moment as a meditation. Here are some **examples**:

Eating

This one area of your life could have the greatest impact of all if you bring consciousness to it. The reason being that the state of a person's consciousness affects the choices of food that they consume and the amounts. Just think of it this way: if you are fully conscious when choosing what you eat and also at the time of eating, you will be operating out of your fundamental nature, which will obviously guide you way better than your programmed nature. Your body already knows what it needs and how much it needs, but the problem is that you have been so blinded by society's norms that you have lost touch with this body wisdom, and now you eat when others do and choose whatever food is most popular. Do you think your super-sophisticated human machine doesn't know what is good for it and when it should eat it? If you doubt your body's innate wisdom, you are very mistaken. Your body is constantly giving you signals and speaking to you, but when you're not conscious or connected to any signals, you mimic the actions of others—like a zombie searching for a brain.

Driving

Since humans seem to always be driving somewhere, why not add some meditation to this part of your day as well? Instead of doing your typical thing, such as blasting music, talking on the phone, cursing at other drivers, or replaying stories in your head, try to just observe yourself throughout your whole drive. Notice the drivers, notice your sensations in your body, notice anytime thoughts are trying to suck you into their story, notice the scenery, notice your reactions to road situations, etc.

If you start adding just a little bit of presence here, rather than being stuck in your mind, you will start noticing that driving can be a very peaceful practice and actually a great way to connect to who you really are.

Daily Errands

Use activities like washing dishes, cooking, cleaning, doing laundry, talking on the phone, mailing something, getting gas, walking, waiting, interacting, etc., to observe how you are doing all these things, how you are feeling, the thoughts that are coming up, and anything else that is in the present moment. Observe yourself as much as you can, without judgement, or any other mind-added things. Just start letting things be, without adding your drama to them.

For **example**, if you are folding clothes, feel how each fabric feels when you touch it, smell the scent, and really be in each moment of folding. What a typical person does in this kind of scenario is think up a storm about anything that has happened already, or might happen later; they become angry that they have many clothes to fold. Use your daily activities to notice your internal state and how little things can change your peace. Always try to get back to the present moment and into your senses, as those are in reality.

Work

Since this takes up most of your time during the day, try to use certain moments at work to check in with yourself as often as possible; observe everything that you can notice in the present moment. If you are new to meditation and this kind of awareness, for the majority of your day you likely will be so stuck in your mental stories that you won't even notice and remember to check in. Of course, some jobs are more rigorous than others and you might not have as much time to check in, but there are always moments—especially if you are serious enough about your peace.

When you are checking in with yourself at work, try to notice how you feel when your boss is telling you to do things, or if you are worried or anxious about a presentation or a report, how you act with coworkers; are you authentic or are you always pretending? Notice your attitude when you go to work; are you miserable to be there or do you choose to be excited? All these types of questioning observations can trigger you back to present-moment consciousness if you are willing.

Just remember that when you are not running in your fully connected and conscious mode, you are operating in a state that isn't optimum—the Zombie Mode. If you are in Zombie Mode eight hours a day, this can have some very strong consequences on your health. Always get back in the present moment, and operate from there as often as you can. When you get taken over by mind stuff, notice, and return to being present and peaceful within.

Social Gatherings

If you are particularly sensitive to energies, you may find it challenging to go out to social events, as your emotions really come in here. You feel all types of energetic sensations inside your body, your programmed neurons fire, your emotions kick into overdrive, and your mind supplies stories to explain them. I have a ton of this kind of experience as I am more on the introverted side. If this is what you feel a lot of the time when attending social events—with family, at work, or in random gatherings—then social activity supplies a prime opportunity to connect to yourself. When you can get fully present in the moment, you will quickly start dissolving the hold that emotions have on you. It isn't easy at first, but the key is being committed to being connected to your senses and being in the now. The answer to your social problems here is being present—because the main reason you are feel social anxiety is because your mind is comparing, analyzing, calculating, and playing back all types of things that may happen or that have happened before. As you are not in the past, and you are not in the future, then what the hell are you worried or anxious about? As Ram Das famously said, be here now.

Set your intention before you even go into a social situation. Once you are at the gathering, try to continue being present in every single moment; be engaged with every single person you interact with. As you do this, try to remain the observer of yourself and your internal condition. Have some attention in your mental processes, as you have to talk, but try to also be the empty not-knowing, but observing, space—which will invite others to be themselves. The main thing to be aware of is that the ego will try to compete in places such as this. After all, there are a lot of people and your ego definitely is not okay with being the worst in the crowd. Try to notice this happening in real time; try to notice how other people's egos will jockey for power by trying to compete with others—about the information that they know, or achievements, etc. The more you get into this experiment, the more your awareness will expand and you will be able to recognize all this happening in real time, and you will also be able to let this go, as you are no longer concerned with feeding your ego, as this is not your fundamental nature. Only people who have not touched this pureness of themselves will chronically need to gain power from others.

Events/Competitions

Are outer things distracting you and making you feel stressed, worried, or anxious? Notice how you feel when you are at a moment of competition, or testing, or a change in your life. Notice how you take on this thing and especially all the sensations and restrictions that your mind throws at you—things like you are not good enough, or it is scary, or why is it happening to you? These are all mind-created stories and they are consuming you—even more so when you place a higher value in an event. I can relate majorly, as I played competitive tennis, and my mind and emotions would hardly ever allow me to compete at my most optimal level. The worst part is that you can practice, study, and prepare as many hours as it takes, but if you have not done some kind of training to turn off the mind (some athletes and performers do learn to so trust their preparation that they can then surrender to the moment, despite their mind habits, allowing them to experience "flow"), when your mind takes a hold of you and the emotions come in, it won't matter the work you have done—because you won't be in the present moment to use that information. You will be consumed in thinking of all the possible outcomes that can happen when you lose, or fail, or mess up, or whatever other thing your mind habitually shows you.

Nature

Try to take time to get out into nature and just observe all the things going on inside you, all the sensations, emotions, thoughts, attitude, etc. Always work on being present in the moment, not getting sucked into things, but always observing. Notice, also, the differences you feel when you are surrounded by natural things, as opposed to manmade things or other people.

Nature is one of the best antidotes to being overwhelmed by your mind and consumed by emotions. In nature things are just being, not doing. They are always in their natural form, particularly if they have limited contact with humans. Make it a habit to hang out in natural settings. Abandon your phone for the whole time you are there. Give yourself fifteen minutes at least to just recharge without any distractions.

Technology

As we live in a world consumed and run by technology, notice how that makes you feel. Notice the sensations inside your body as you watch TV or use your computer or phone. Are you letting things that you read or look at affect your inner peace? Notice if your mind makes you believe that you are unworthy in the context of all the information that you're imbibing. Really notice social networks; many people get caught up in the competition game, looking at others' pictures, friends, or posts and then needing to post their own virtual life. It's okay if you enjoy this, but is your mind sucking you into this or are you doing it because you enjoy it? Notice if you are overtaken by this and you can't even live without posting something. If it is for work, then it may be mandatory, but if it's just you needing to post something for others to see, then you might want to question if you are forced by your mind to do this. If it has become an addiction.

The key with all this practice is to notice if you are being pushed around, or are you mostly in control and able to decide to not do something?

Relationships

This could be one of the most powerfully transformative areas of this experiment, as we are constantly involved in interactions throughout our day. Relationships can be with your partner, your family member, your friends, your pets, etc. All these relationships can be used as your practice. The biggest thing to realize here is that everybody is different, and to your ego this is a problem. Your ego compares, judges, analyzes, calculates, and when the results are not to its liking, it makes a big deal of it and causes you suffering of some kind. Your inner state changes and you get into all sorts of dramas with people or with yourself about those people. Notice this in your relationships today, and try to become the space for other beings just to exist without your mind getting involved. The key here is for you to stay at peace within yourself, no matter what is going on externally. **Example:** if you don't agree with another person on something, or if they didn't do what they promised to, or if they treated you in a way you thought wasn't right, all these types of situations can lead to the change of your inner state from peaceful to angry, frustrated, annoyed, etc. The real truth is that it is what it is, and you can let it change your peace or you can accept it and allow it to be. I am not saying you have to be happy; you can still express your opinion, but in a conscious way. Also, understand that many people are unconscious throughout their day, and acting out of their Zombie Mode, so they don't even notice they are hurting you, as they are suffering themselves. When you start fighting them, you just add ammo to their ego and a battle occurs.

Really work on this area. This can lead to you having very deep relationships with others if you realize that you and they are the same. Notice how you feel when you interact with others, notice if you get consumed by your thoughts, notice the programs that start operating you. Try to really be the observer in your relationships. Once you can do this, you will be able to dissolve many unnecessary fights or disagreements. You will also be able to connect more deeply to people, as you will be able to notice what is happening in them, and in their most fundamental nature. Whoever they are to you, they are still an infinite being at their core, just like you; they are merely stuck in Zombie Mode, and either don't know that it is happening or don't know how to stop it. Ask yourself if a joyful person would act like an evil monster. Probably not. Would you act like an evil monster if you were joyous? Then probably they are suffering at some level. Yes, you may be suffering at some level too. (Now notice if you are happy I added this for you, to make you feel better. If you are happy, that's your ego wanting some acknowledgement for its suffering.)

In this part of the investigation, you are trying to observe yourself, as this will show you how you are programmed in everything. Once you start noticing these programs occurring, you can start changing them. This is self-mastery and it will be your journey to the new you.

Tip:

A great help in all of these areas is the ability to be able to dis-identify with your mental activity and even from your body at any moment. In doing so, you gain your power back— all the drama will then just be occurring in the background as you watch all that is.

You are not the body or mind—stop being duped that you are by continuing to be totally identified by them. This is a trap. Create space—create peace. Use the present moment to do this.

Getting Captured

I will describe some symptoms you will experience when you have been captured in Zombie Mode. You will be captured often, and that is the main reason you should work on this experiment. Being aware when symptoms hit gives you the ability to wake up, rather than get taken over—sometimes for hours, sometimes for days, sometimes for months.

Symptoms of Zombie Mode: feeling unworthy, rushed, anxious, stressed, worried, angry, in pain, suffering, frustrated, judgmental, detached from others, lost, depressed, suicidal, etc.

This Zombie switch happens very quickly and the problem is that you most likely will not notice this until you have been feeling any one or multiple of these symptoms. Symptoms can be triggered by any moment, but mostly moments that the mind doesn't like.

Sometimes these moments will be easy to spot and other times not. The key to recognizing them is always to have some of your attention in your internal state, rather than be consumed by your mind. If you have some awareness of your internal state, you will be able to dissolve the mind's stories fairly quickly, as they will not have time to gather momentum and consumed you fully. Once you have been fully captured, you most likely will be acting out your zombie ways in the physical world. You might get angry at some person, you might be angry at yourself, you might treat your pet or kids in a mean way, you might want to do something destructive to yourself or others, you might try to want to suppress your feelings by taking drugs, you might try to distract yourself with anything really.

The instant you spot that you aren't conscious, try to put your attention in the present moment and into your senses. Allow anything that you feel to be as it is, and don't go back inside your head and play mind games about how this shouldn't be happening and why it is happening to you.

The more often you are able to spot that you have been switched to Zombie Mode, the more your awareness starts to build, and eventually you will be able to start noticing as you are about to get captured by your mind. This is what we are working on: living in real time, in the present moment. When you can do this, then you will always be able to put some attention into your internal state of being, instead of getting all your attention consumed by your mental processes.

Basically you are trying to be an entity that observes all that is going on inside and outside. Yes, of course you can still allow yourself to get consumed by things, such as a relationship, an event, a competition, etc., but you can then quickly realize that you have had your full attention there and not in your inner state.

Try to realize that the most important thing in your life is how your internal state is. If you are always connected and peaceful, you will always be operating at your highest potential. If you are disconnected from your fundamental nature, you will get consumed by your ego and it needs a lot of extras to keep you happy.

REALIZATIONS

Distorted Truth

100 Realizations

Now that I've told you how to start this experiential journey, I will list and explain as clearly as possible some of the things that have come to me just by allowing them to arise in the empty space of meditation. You all can have these and many other realizations once you start this process. Just experiencing these realizations has changed my life and brought me to much greater heights, as I can see the world through a clearer lens than the one that has been programmed onto me.

These are not listed in any particular order.

1. Enlightenment

Are you guys aware of what enlightenment is, and that you can achieve this in your life? Or I should say, switch to this, because it's already there for you. You don't have to be a monk or a guru or any other hokey pokey to reach this state. You just need to really put in some time in order to dig out from the rubble what it is that you truly are.

Most people go through their whole life just focusing on achievements and gaining possessions on the physical world—which is an obviously needed step in our existence—but they never really go beyond this.

After you go through all the primary stages in development (think Maslow), there needs to be a time when you start turning inward and learning how to get back to your purest form and live from there.

This is by no means a mandatory step, as some people are totally okay with having their focus on physical things for the rest of their life. Although, if your goal is to have meaning and learn how to operate at your highest level, then you might want to consider working on this at least part time.

When you start working on this journey, the biggest thing that changes is your level of awareness, which affects how you see the world and yourself. You might think it isn't worth the effort, but let me tell you, our ego fools us into thinking we know a lot, yet we know so very little.

2. Attachment/Detachment

Try to remember the earliest moment of your life . . . Okay, you got that memory? Well, even earlier than that time, you were getting attached to things on this planet, and this attachment has been going on up to the present.

Sure, you also detached from some things, but the detachment has been very minimal, and mostly happened because the thing broke, or you outgrew it, or it just didn't work out.

The key is to learn how to detach from outer things for even just a little time, and on your own—before you are forced to let go of them. If you are able to do this on your own, it will cause you a lot less suffering when it's time to let a thing go for real. When you can detach from something before it is taken from you, your perspective will automatically change as well, because you get to see the view outside of your attachment. This is such a huge deal because when you are attached to something, you are always blinded by it.

This is true with anything: relationships, jobs, kids, etc. All these things are ultimately not you, which means that there will come a time when you will need to be able to detach from those things. I don't mean to suggest that you should give away your kids or husband (ha ha, although you might really want to at times). I just mean that they are additions as well, and if you think that without those things you couldn't exist, then you're going to have a hard time letting go when you have to.

All beings are the universe expressing itself through their form, and just because you own something or even gave birth to it does not mean it is ultimately yours. You're just having an experience with it.

Attach yourself fully to things, but also learn how to detach. But be aware that just detaching and being scared to attach is not good either; being scared of anything is a clue that Zombie Mode has taken over. Knowing how to peacefully attach and detach is the key.

3. Love

What I have noticed in our society is that since many people are run by their minds, even the love that they hold for others is affected by their minds. True love is feeling the connection that you and another being are ultimately one and not separate.

What seems to be happening on our planet today is people feel some feelings, and then once those wear off, the mind comes in and takes over. It deludes us into thinking that love is felt through the separate ego. You then only love people when they do stuff for you or it's convenient to you, and if your ego isn't satisfied your "love" goes away.

Notice in your relationships, if you are constantly wanting the person you love to be a certain way, do things in a certain manner, dress and look up to your standards. These are all egoic desires and having them satisfied will only please you for a second, and your ego will quickly want your partner to fit your new standards.

Try to totally accept your partner for who they are, without changing them. The beauty is that everyone is different and when you allow them to be them, and they allow you to be you, you fully experience the beauty. Really try to work on connecting to your fundamental nature, so your love can be intensified due to you again feeling that oneness with yourself, and then it is reflected to others.

Be aware that although you might have true love for another, they may be captured by their ego. Don't judge them as bad. Just try to stay fully present and conscious to not feed their zombie. Of course, if the person is too far turned and not ready to work on themselves, then you might need to get out of the relationship. You will still love their true nature, but their Zombie Mode might be too much.

4. Vibrations/Frequencies

Notice today, in your own experience, that you have a vibrational state and so does everything. Now once you've got that, you have to be aware that anything can change your vibrations if you aren't present enough. This can happen with contact to a person, an event, a thing, a memory, a thought, etc.

This usually happens discreetly because you aren't aware of this, and perhaps you have never been able to get outside of your mind enough to experience it. Usually people only notice after the vibrational change has

manifested into something more physical in
their experience.

Try getting more in tune with yourself by
meditating or doing yoga, as such things help
your awareness expand and help you notice more
things inside and outside of yourself.

We operate at different frequencies.
Notice your frequency at its highest level
(days when you're feeling empowered and
operating at ease), and also notice when you
are at its lowest level (days when you are
struggling with everything).

The biggest difference, if you actually
take time to observe this, is that, at low
frequency, your mind has attached with emotions
and has become super powerful and energy gets
blocked instead of flowing through your whole
body, the way it does at high frequency. Notice
these low-frequency symptoms and put your
awareness in the problem area, allowing it to
dissolve the tension and block.

To do this, you have to be present and
fully in your senses. Otherwise you won't even
feel the vibrations; you will just complain
about something bothering you.

5. Self-Acceptance

A term that is not existent for the ego. From
your egoic point of view, notice that there are

no perfect beings on this planet—including you. You must prove to your ego time and again that you are worthy, and you must listen to its insults throughout your day.

This is probably familiar torture. The mind tells us: you're not good enough; you're ugly; this isn't right; you're too short; you're too tall; your nose sticks out; why aren't you smarter; why aren't you prettier; that person is so gorgeous, why am I a gargoyle, etc.

Well, if you are tired of that life and want to start noticing that you are actually the most perfect, beautiful being, then start letting go of your fake identity and the picture it has created for you to live up to, and realize that you came perfect the way you are.

Start accepting that you are the only copy of you, and you were designed perfectly, but this voice eventually came in and started saying all this nonsense to you, and now you're confused. Everyone is perfectly designed because it's the one thing that we humans have no say or control in, yet.

We grew in this body and we can appreciate it—unless you're a lunatic, in which case you may blame your parents for giving you this body, like they chose theirs as well, and so on. Don't play the victim game (it's the ego). Use what you have in the best, most

conscious manner. Enjoy life by accepting
yourself fully and being connected to the
truest nature of yourself, which is outside of
all labels.

6. Old Age

A term in today's society that can be
interchanged with the word "broken."

Witness how society today is very
unconscious and all we really care about is
money, success, and staying younger forever. If
your main focus in life is how to look younger
because you're scared of what others will think
if you have some wrinkles, then you have to
start meditating full time.

Start enjoying the present moment and
whatever age you are. Age is just to help us
keep track of things.

We perceive aging as a bad thing, and
instead of using it to start detaching from who
we are not, we try to cling to things even
more. It's okay if you don't remember things as
you once did; that's the point—those memories
aren't you. It's okay if you can't move the way
you once did; you've been rushing your whole
life; slow down!

When we are young, we wish to be older,
and when we are older to be younger. How about
you stop wishing and just experience the beauty

of your life at every stage you are in? Be aware that existence is trying to show you to let go and start allowing what is to be. Aging can be an amazing thing, when you stop believing all the stupid morons telling you otherwise.

Obviously you're going to go through challenges, but at what part of your life was that not the case?

7. Death - Part 1

Have you ever contemplated your own death? If you're like most people, then probably not! Probably you are afraid of death and don't even want to think what happens when it happens. In society we get taught that death is horrible, and if it were possible to get implanted into robot bodies just to stay alive longer, it seems like many people would do it.

The thing is that most people don't even live lives that they enjoy, because it seems like they are too scared to and think they have a lot of time left. But in honesty, you don't. You might be dead the next second, minute, or day, so start realizing that and using death as a push to get out of your unconscious state daily. Start doing things you want to be doing, instead making excuses and being afraid of others' judgments and whatever else you are hiding from.

To the ego, death means the end, and it decides to take it upon itself to control your life by being afraid to live. Kill your ego now, so you can finally begin to live fully.

If you start connecting to your fundamental nature by doing this experiment, then you will start seeing life and death in the same picture—not as one being better than the other. If you go really deep within, you can even see that death is actually just an illusion. Contemplating death will be of tremendous help especially when you start getting into your older years. Many elderly people live mostly in the past, as they see death as the end. Why ever live that way?

Death - Part 2

When others die, realize that the only thing that is suffering is the mind you, not your fundamental self.

The person that has died isn't suffering; it's the you that has become so attached to the ideas, memories, and beliefs that were created by your mind about the other human. You don't want to let go of your mind creation because you've made a self out of it. A part of your created self is based on that other and now you suffer because your facade is being exposed. One character from your fiction novel has been removed.

The funny part is that they're fine, the being went back to source (oneness). It's quite crazy how deceptive and genius this is actually. Start learning to detach from what you are not (mind self) and the way you will start seeing and dealing with death and loss will be a lot more real.

See, the you that you think you are currently, needs all the characters around because it depends on them, your real being doesn't need them, it knows what they are, the same way it knows what you are. This can be experienced and it needs to be if one wants true understanding.

You can still feel sad and cry because that's part of the realism of this story, but always remember that actual truth or you might just let this affect the rest of your time here on earth and even make it seem as if you are doing them a favor by not letting go. The only favor your doing is to your mind created self and it will thank you with tons of suffering.

8. Seed

An object that seems to be so small, yet when cared for in the proper manner, produces the most amazing results. Try to notice today in your own experience that your dreams and ideas are like seeds; they pop out of you and then you can use your thoughts to create movement,

which helps the seeds to grow and manifest.
Unfortunately most people's minds are full of
barriers and they don't create movement; they
block their seeds.

Try to plant your seeds and see what kind
of limitations your mind puts on them. Really
notice the reasons you tell yourself why
something can't manifest for you. And then ask
yourself why you believe these reasons, and are
they true? It's funny all the things we tell
ourselves about our inability to create,
despite the fact that so many things have been
created by others already.

Realize that even literal seeds have
obstacles occurring all the time, such as a
lack of water, too much water, heavy winds,
animals, bugs, etc.

You can't and don't have to force things
to manifest. Do whatever is possible each day
that you are in your present moment, and allow
things to be as well. Most regular people don't
help plants to grow normally, right? Like, they
don't get in the dirt, grab the little seeds,
yank, and stretch them to bloom. And even if
they could do this—grab a tiny stem and yank
it—the plant probably wouldn't survive it. So
stop trying to control everything with your
dreams and ideas as well.

9. Levels of Separation

Have you ever noticed the levels of separation that we have as humans? It would be great if, once we are old enough, someone gave us all a briefing, saying, "Okay, these are some categories we have put you in. Make sure to not take them so seriously, as they are absolutely not you!" and then they kept reinforcing that. Unfortunately that hasn't happened, and now tons of people are stuck believing that they are those things. Not so bad or harmful, you may think, but what happens when other people believe their labels and those labels differ and conflict with yours? Well, we already do know what happens. It's called today.

Here are just some simple categories we are put into without our control:

First, you are categorized as a boy or a girl, name, then your color, then your size, then your country, looks, smarts, height, school, family, wealth, etc. Those are just obvious categories. How about more deceptive ones, such as our personality?

Can you see that all these levels of categories get you further and further from your fundamental nature? What are you outside of these things? Have you searched or questioned who you are—even outside of your name? You obviously aren't your name, as that was given to you, but we hold it very firmly as ourselves.

The more and more you start dis-
identifying with the stuff gathered, the sooner
you experience what your fundamental nature is.
You may be thinking, Why should I waste my time
searching when I can't understand what I am?
But you are assuming that your true nature is
something to understand. Who you are can be an
experience that is outside of your mind.

Some people get a glimpse of their pure
essence, but it's usually by accident, and they
have no clue what is going on, it doesn't last
very long, and they get sucked back into the
categories and to "normal" life.

10. Real

Try to do an experiment today for yourself
instead of going about your day the customary
way. Try to only put attention on what is real
in each moment. The way you can do this is by
only paying attention to what you are touching,
smelling, tasting, seeing, and hearing.

If it is not in your direct experience,
do not give it attention at all.

Example: If you're going to drive to some
destination, only focus on the real moment of
that journey, not mind stuff! Once you've made
a decision, use only your senses and try to
feel as many of them in every moment as you
can. Get specific . . . feel yourself walking
to your car, opening the door, getting into

your seat, touching the steering wheel, putting on the seatbelt, turning the key, etc. Don't skip these events, because if you do, you're somewhere else. Do this your whole journey and while you are driving, keeping focus only on the things perceived by your senses, and don't let your mind take over your attention. If you notice that you're feeling rushed, that is your mind trying to sneak in.

All your sensory experiences are the most real, so if you stick with those as often as you can, you're getting the most real picture of life.

You have to be vigilant though, because mostly we listen to our mind stuff and what it tells us about the sensations—rather than noticing "soft," the mind says, "Boy, I'm really noticing how soft the seat is." This is like watching an animal show with narration. Yes, it's entertaining and it seems to be what is going on in the picture, but it's totally made up. The guy narrating can make the saddest story or the most joyful, and then we believe it. Well, this is the same thing that you do all day long by imposing your mental stories onto what you experience.

11. Money

The object that we all want more than anything, yet at the same time it causes the most problems on our planet. Have you ever taken the time to really look at what money is, and the relationship you have with it?

Many people put a huge value on money and they struggle with it a lot, but if you really look at what it really is, you will see that it's some paper and some metal. Money has no real value. So if you're struggling with it, try to realize that the value is in the service or item that you need, or that you think you need. If you look at it this way, rather than worshiping it, you can start to be more relaxed about it.

If you need or want more money, the same principles apply. If you can master a particular skill that others can use, or you can create something that others will need, then there's a good chance that they will trade the paper and metal for your skill or item.

Every single person can offer something, and this is what you have to figure out for yourself: what can you offer so that you can start contributing to the planet in your best and most enjoyable manner?

Also, try to start observing what you are doing in your life, because most people work jobs that they don't really like, just to buy things that they don't really need. Are you just going by what society and your ego wants? Or are you actually taking the time to look inside yourself for what you need and what will fulfill you?

12. Past

It is amazing that as humans we have the ability to remember past events, but it is even more amazing all the time most humans spend in those events rather than in present-moment reality. Try to notice today if you live a lot of your life in the past. Many people get captured by past events (good or bad), and they compare every situation to them. Having your attention captured constantly by the past will leave you with a lot of worry.

Right now, try to capture this happening inside yourself. If you notice it once, you can be more aware of it happening in other moments. The cure for worry is to get out of your thinking and back into your senses in the present moment.

You have to remember that each moment is its own moment, and you have to give it the attention in the moment that it is happening— rather than once it has passed into memory.

Your ego loves using the past to create all types of crazy stories for you. The problem is that you get stuck in them and believe them like they are true. Use the past to learn in some instances, but don't get stuck there, especially knowing that the ego's version is altered from the reality that was.

13. Future

The moment in which many humans seek happiness, it is a fictional land where we live out many hours of our day, hoping the next moment will be better than this one. Try to notice today what is going on in your head. If you pay attention without getting caught in your thoughts, you will notice that you are living a lot of your life in the future. You fantasize, you act out, you fear, you plan, etc., all types of things in your head.

Recognize that you do this all day long, and the worst part is that you don't know how to stop it. You might think you do, but in the next moment, you already have been caught in another future thought. This is the primary reason you are anxious in life. How can you not be, when you are thinking stuff up, and then trying to solve the thing that you just thought up?

Every time you are in the future, your attention goes to that moment, so guess who's operating you in the present moment. It's your programs (Zombie Mode). These are the programs that have been downloaded onto you from as early as childhood.

This is your ego's genius plan. It distracts you with things to think about, while it runs the real show in the present. Use the future to plan things, but switch to the present moment, or you are going to be living in constant anxiety. This is a human disease, cure yourself!

14. Joyfulness

A state of being where you don't need outer events or objects to make you happy; mere existence is more than enough. Can you feel joy without needing things to happen for you, or gaining possessions? Most people seem like they can't, because they've lost touch with what joy really is.

They constantly need the next event and next new item or their mind goes into overdrive. If you start detaching from your fake self and touching your true nature, you will then be able to again feel joy for life. It's an amazing feeling, and if you want any sort of real happiness, you should start working on this.

Every one of you has felt this joy growing up, but then it gets hidden when your mind comes into full power, and many people unfortunately never get it back. It's really sad actually, so try to at least learn to switch from your mind to just being still once in a while; then you'll have some balance.

Real joy always comes in the now; it's you realizing that you are lucky enough to be experiencing this unbelievable reality that exists for you.

15. The Body Is Finite, but You Are Infinite

You are an infinite being, but your physical body is temporary. As humans, we seek infinity in the physical world because this is all we really know. You can see how we are never really satisfied with anything; always wanting more and more and more.

If you can understand that nothing will ever fully satisfy you on the physical world—since things are temporary here—then you can start finding fulfillment by touching your infinite nature which lies within. If you touch this, by removing all that is not you, you then can enjoy physical life as you know it's temporary, and you can detach a lot more easily from it than a person who thinks that all that they are is this physical entity.

You can't just know this intellectually either; it won't help much. You need to do the work and start separating from your ego to experience purely your infinite nature.

16. Movement

Have you ever taken the time to notice all the sensations that are moving inside your body? Try not to think about them, but just observe as many of these sensations as you can. These are all happenings that are occurring for you in the present moment.

The problem with most people is that they feel these sensations going on inside them, but instead of accepting them as they are, floating around, their mind decides to label them as if it knows what they are.

Isn't it kind of weird that we just accept that the mind knows things like that?

Also, have you ever decided to just go totally toward those sensations and feel them fully? Probably not, as your mind scares you away from doing such a thing. Some people are so caught up in thoughts all day long, that they aren't even aware that when you put your attention on your senses, you can notice all this movement going on.

Get to know this movement inside you, and start connecting to it, and observing all that you feel without any explanation from your mind, or wanting different sensations. If you start doing this, you will get closer and closer to understanding yourself, and it will be outside of your mind's conceptualizations.

If we are energy, and energy is movement, then at your core you are this movement, no? If this is true, then wouldn't the movement of all these sensations be more the truth of you than just the made-up mind descriptions that we've downloaded from other humans?

17. Reactions

A conscious or unconscious act done in response to something. Try to be aware that the reactions you have to an event, person, situation, etc., can show you how conscious and present you are. By observing your reactions, you will see that many things can cause you to automatically act from your programmed self, which is an automatic response, when you are stuck in your mind and not living in the now.

If you are okay with this, that's fine, but if you want to grow and not be controlled by your programs, then you can use your automatic reactions to see what you have to work on.

For **example**, you come home and your dog peed in the house. Automatically you might get angry, annoyed, and maybe even hit your dog because of this behavior. The question is, was this your choosing? Mostly your Zombie Mode took you over and you acted like this because of conditioning (A Program).

Be aware of your reactions as you act them out, and if you are unable to witness that quickly, then reflect on your reactions after the fact. If you keep doing this, eventually you will be able to have enough awareness to simultaneously witness and act out. Don't get angry at yourself for acting like this. Know that by spotting your Zombie Mode reactions quicker and quicker, you will eventually be able to spot them fast enough to stop acting out.

18. Battle (You vs. You)

If you have had times when you were able to separate from your mind briefly, then you have witnessed that the biggest battle in your whole life has always been, and continues to be, you versus you. The problem is that your mind makes you believe the battle is you versus other. This is why humans do the things that they do to other people, the environment, other beings, themselves, etc.

When you are in a constant daily battle within, how can you expect to run in a smooth manner?

Unfortunately most people are sucked into and captured by mind-made fiction, so they project their struggles onto and battle external events and people, as if they are the source of the problems.

Start seeing the true battle you're in, and fight it from the source. Master yourself from within.

19. Decisions

What should I do? Did I choose right? I need more information to decide.

Have you ever witnessed that no matter how much data you gather about a certain event or situation, you will never be able to gather enough. There are infinite possibilities for everything, things that you can't ever even expect, which means that your decisions will never be "perfect."

Sure, it's nice to prepare for things when you can, but notice if, when making decisions, your mind is useful or just consumes you with all types of crazy nonsense throughout your day and even weeks. Use your mind to think when needed, but notice if you then can let go and be present in all the other things that you're doing in the now.

Try to connect to your truest nature by getting into your senses and being in the present moment and asking yourself if this decision is something that will make you ultimately happy or move you in that direction. If you feel like it's not right, then there is your answer.

Make sure you don't make a decision only to allow the mind to second guess and punish you: "See? I told you that was a dumb decision!" Whatever you decide, accept it, and any outcome can seem bad at first, and then ultimately lead you in the right direction.

20. Relationships

Try to use a relationship that you have with somebody today—a friend, a family member, or a partner—to notice your unconscious behavior.

Notice when you react in Zombie Mode, but don't be egoic about your observations; no calling yourself an unconscious monster who ought be able to just snap out of it. Simply notice what triggers your Zombie Mode reactions. See when this happens, how often, and how long it lasts.

If you haven't worked on this, it may be difficult at first. But here are some common situations:

Waiting in lines, if a cashier is taking too long, traffic jams, running late, the cable/internet does work or is slow, you missed a show, kid tantrums, not recognized for work done by a boss, car breaks down, favorite clothes get ruined, asked to stay longer at work.

The list is endless, but I'm sure you get the gist.

Basically anything that has the power to turn a person from human into a zombie is a potential trigger situation. Once you can notice others switching, then notice when it happens to you. Really be aware how your behavior changes and how you act out through unconscious programs. Some people are almost always unconscious, and this might be the case for you as well, so be aware of this too.

If most of your interactions are complaining about others, how work sucks, and how your life is miserable, then look at this as signs that you are being constantly triggered into Zombie Mode. The more you can see your own reactions and eventually disconnect enough to diffuse them, the more okay you will be with other people being and turning unconscious. You will observe this without getting sucked into it yourself. Also, don't start judging other's as unconscious, as that is a clever little game your ego will try to play to feel superior. Ultimately unconscious people are not worse than you; they just forgot what their true nature is, and they are operating in their mind-made self, which constantly needs to be fed to feel worthy.

21. Blind Momentum

Try to notice in your experience today if when you build momentum in a particular area in your life—such as acting on an idea or a goal that you want to accomplish—it blinds you from other things. Your mind takes over and keeps you stuck in this thing and tunnel vision occurs. You then don't focus on other areas of your life because you are captured by the momentum.

Many people get so consumed that their relationships crumble, their health is affected, their eating doesn't matter, and so on. Momentum can be a great thing, and some people could use more of it. But you know you are at the mercy of blind momentum if, even when you do achieve your goal, not only does it not satisfy you as much as you thought it would, but also you become almost depressed as you finally notice that so many other things took a hit.

Try to maintain a vision of the whole picture, with every aspect of your life, because everything is connected and if you just focus and get blinded by one item's momentum, it can damage other areas. Here is an **example:** Imagine yourself running away from a giant boulder falling downhill. If all that you care about is getting away from this boulder, you might not notice that there is a cliff at the bottom and, even though you don't get hit by the boulder, you die by falling over the side of the cliff.

This happens as well with relationships. People get obsessed with each other because things are fresh and new, and all of a sudden they're married and it's been like a month, and eventually when the momentum wares off, they realize that they were so consumed that they didn't see the whole picture.

22. Four Ways

Notice right now that there are at least four ways that you can go beyond your physical self:

Silence

Stillness

Emptiness

Nothing

There may be more ways, but these are the ways that I observed to connect beyond the physical to my fundamental nature.

By putting your full attention into any one of these four ways—without the help of your mind, as that is the one thing that is preventing you from experiencing who you really are—you can then touch something beyond physical you which cannot be explained by words, but can be shown to you by the amount of peace and love that floods you and radiates from you.

What do these four ways have in common?
They cannot be claimed and they exist always.
No matter what is going on, all these things
are there for you if you just pay attention to
them.

Try focusing on one of these four ways
for a couple of minutes with as much attention
as you can give and notice how you feel
afterwards. Do this especially when you are
super stuck in your mind's grip.

If you're feeling small and unworthy,
this is the way to change that as well.

23. Sounds

Have you ever observed sounds on a deeper
level? If you have, you would have noticed that
sounds come from nothing and go back into
nothing. You might be like, Okay, cool, what
the heck is this guy talking about? The thing
is that "nothing" is the key here, but you need
the sound to notice the "nothing."

Nothing exists everywhere around us, but
we don't notice it because we think it's just
useless, and when something is everywhere, we
don't pay attention to it. Try to use sounds
today to actually connect to this nothing,
because that's where your true self resides,
and you have access to this always, but you
need to put your attention on it.

It is easiest to use a sound that comes and goes to notice this nothing. Focus your attention on when the sound ends or just before it begins, to really be able to witness it and feel the calmness and peace that comes with it. When you're overtaken with the chaos of life, you can use this technique to touch your true, peaceful nature.

24. Suffering

Suffering may come in many forms and occur in all types of situations—suffering through anger, fear, pain, frustration, annoyance, etc.

All these things happen because you've lost touch with your true nature and don't accept reality to be as it is. Your mind takes over your peace and the ego makes you into a victim. Now you play all types of stories for yourself, instead of just dealing with reality.

Example: If your car breaks down, why do you need to make a big deal of it? Don't cars break down all the time in reality? Well, but now it happened to you, all mighty egoic you, and this is terrible and should have never happened. But this is Zombie Mode suffering.

Notice anytime you are suffering and link it back to the root problem, the mind. Yes, things will occur sometimes that aren't that great, but you can do what you can to resolve them in the now, and then let them go. Fighting reality isn't a great solution, as you will always lose. Be aware of this and try to start using suffering as a way to snap out of Zombie Mode.

Once you are able to see this inside you, you can then witness when others try to bring you into their suffering. Unconscious people will spend a lot of their time complaining about others and trying to feed off of you by bringing you into their stories. Don't get caught in this trap. Be the observer of yourself while you interact with others and always keep some attention in your internal state.

25. Competition

Competition is a major aspect of our world today. It not only exists for you internally, where you are battling the voice in your head, but it can be witnessed in every aspect of society. The major issue is that competition is a mind-made phenomenon, and it's causing you a great deal of suffering. Competition is a by-product of the ego and we use it as a means to determine our success.

Let's say you are an artist and you have been creating artwork for thirty years. You have put your heart, sweat, and tears, into creating these masterpieces. All this time you were living in a cave, but now you decide to go outside. You go to the city and you start seeing all different types of artwork, and all of a sudden your masterpieces that you enjoyed making look like scribbles compared to the other artists' work. You suffer because your mind will tell you your work sucks, and that one is better, and you should quit, and so on.

This is how the ego functions, and instead of letting that happen, do things in the best manner that you can and just enjoy what others create as well. You can compete, but don't use it as a means to determine your success, or you will always lose in the long run; when your ego is in control, you're always going to be a loser.

This holds true in every area of your life, so don't compete against others; just enjoy each moment as you.

26. Energy

Try to start your engine with some movement. Just as a train takes some time to start moving, so do you—especially when you have been stationary or have just awakened. Once you gain momentum (conscious, as opposed to blind momentum), it becomes a lot easier to coast and use the energy flow.

Try to notice this in your actual experience, because when you can see it and not just know about it, it will be a powerful insight to get you through tough times.

This doesn't mean you have to go run a marathon each day. Just get up and take a walk around your street, do some yoga, or whatever else you enjoy. While you're doing that activity, be fully present and enjoy it—but that is another story.

27. Surrender

Which definition do you prefer: the act of totally accepting reality, or, in popular culture, being a coward and giving up?

Are you aware that most of your life you either are battling situations or resisting them? This is because you are going against reality most of the time and not surrendering to what is real. This doesn't mean you don't try to take action and problem solve; it means that you don't blame what is and wish it were different.

Many people make themselves victims and make it seem like everything is against them. The fact of the matter is that things are as they are, and labeling things as bad and good makes you believe that they are, when they are just how they are.

Surrender to things as they are and take action if you can, instead of wasting valuable energy wishing that some things didn't exist, people didn't act the way they do, and so on.

28. Not Knowing

For many people, not knowing something feels like a weakness, and they'd rather pretend to know or make things up, as the judgement of others (who also feel that it is a flaw not to know) is too hard to bear. What I have experienced is that living in a state of not knowing something is way more powerful than thinking you know everything and trying to defend this knowledge.

The ego hates you enjoying not knowing, because if you actually do this, especially in the beginning you will notice that your ego feels weakened—mainly when others flaunt all they know. Suddenly it is losing the competition of who knows more and is therefore more worthy. This is frequently evident in social gatherings, competitions, schools, jobs, etc.

When you start growing and mastering yourself, you need to start letting go of knowing answers and knowledge, because if you really think about it, why the hell would you ever need to prove to someone or to yourself that you know something? And why on earth should not knowing make you feel unworthy? Only your ego needs this; you are perfectly fine not knowing anything!

Of course, it is also okay to gain knowledge in areas and know things, as it is useful on the physical world and can help you live responsibly. But really focus on *why* you're learning, and whether you are using what you learn to better yourself and others or just to compete.

From an empty place of not knowing, you can be open to all possibilities; when you know, you limit yourself.

29. Grounding and Plants

Many people on this planet live isolated from earth's contact for long periods of time. We live in tall, insulated buildings, go to work in artificially made environments, are surrounded with electronics, and always wear shoes.

All this stuff influences how you feel and how disconnected you get from your most natural state. It is important to spend some time in nature for a couple minutes a day, at least to recalibrate your system. You do know that we are literally made of the same matter as the cosmos, right?

Here are two simple things that can help you get some connection: grounding and plants.

Grounding:

Just putting your bare feet or hands on top of the earth (soil, grass, beach, etc.) for a short period of time can help recalibrate your magnetic flow. Try this especially if you land in another time zone; I've found that it helps reduce jet lag.

Plants:

Add some plants inside your house, as just being in the presence of living things can get you out of your mind and connect you back to being.

30. Life Purpose

Have you ever taken the time to look at what makes you REALLY satisfied and what you want to be doing with your life?

Most people are too busy to look, because they are so worried about success, or making money, or they are trapped in the society life style. You might be dead tomorrow. This fact is a good push to get you to start working on things that you absolutely love, and find a way to spend most of your day doing those things!

If you are not passionate about anything, then think back to the time you were a kid and would just do anything that was fun and meaningful to you. Remember what you loved then. What did you love about those things? What can you do right now to have those same experiences?

31. Pain

The one area of life that most humans try to avoid, yet when pain is experienced fully, it can be your ticket out of unconsciousness.

Most people's awareness is very limited, so they cannot spot when they are conscious and unconscious. However, when you are in pain, you can actually use it to turn conscious by being brave and going toward the pain. (If it's something unbearable, then chances are it might be hard for you to do that—as your mind has too much power over you. But if you are feeling some kind of milder pain, then go toward it as fully as you are able.)

To do this, get in your senses in the present moment and go toward the pain even though your unconscious (zombie) mind tells you not to; understand that the ego-embodied zombie wants to live, so it will resist because it doesn't want you to regain your power (consciousness) and kill it.

The biggest problem with pain is the suffering that your mind causes you by making you believe that this shouldn't have happened to you; it may even play back the pain-causing event for you, or play you all sorts of future horror-resultant scenarios. That is all fiction. The present moment is real, so accept it and feel it without your mind drama. When you can face the pain and notice that you're still alive and okay, the mind loses its power for a second.

Try to test this for yourself when you are in pain in some area. Just face reality (the sensation of pain) and don't let your mind take you over fully and add its victim stories. Yes, sometimes things may seem to suck, but still that is real, so face the real, not the millions of stories your mind spins.

32. Lost

Have you ever felt lost?

If so, good! That means you've done more questioning of yourself than most people have done. When you realize that you have no clue what life is, where you are, and what you're doing here, you can finally see that you are not in control of a lot of things in this life, and instead of trying to hold control, you can accept things as they are and not just as you wish them to be.

There are no set structures for how a human being has to live; we try adding them for ourselves, but there are infinite possibilities, and this is why you might be feeling lost a lot of the time. Just continue questioning your motivation, and do what best suits you, not what others just tell you to do, or things that you see commonly.

33. Receiving

The process of being so in tune with your body that you are able to notice even the most subtle sensations coming in from source energy. Otherwise you're mostly receiving brainwashing propaganda.

Get out of your head for a second and go beyond conceptual knowledge, which means go beyond thoughts, labels, beliefs, programs, etc., and receive pure intelligence. This channel is open for you at every moment; you just need to connect to it by taking your attention out of your mind and putting it into your body.

34. Do Do Head

Try to notice today in your own direct experience that society is in the business of doing things and you are sucked into that doing as well. Your whole life consists of doing and doing and doing (you are a Do Do Head). When do you just be life? Like actually experience fully the reality of this existence at this moment without an agenda?

We are given this amazing ability to be so connected to life that we actually become it fully. The self goes away and you become all.

When you're just stuck as a Do Do Head, reality become deader and deader, you see things still, but through so many layers that you really don't even see. Truth doesn't exist in the mind and with a self.

Start being, it's the most joyful and powerful way of living life. You then start doing things, but they all come out of being. This way consciousness and you unite and create through love. Unconsciousness is already shown to us everywhere in this world, it obviously isn't working anymore for the human race. Our world is full of Do Do Heads, all doing things constantly to solve the world's problems, yet violence, hate, and unhappiness exist more everywhere than ever before.

Solution = Being

35. Spying

Most people are not aware that you can separate yourself from your thinking and you can spy/observe your daily patterns. You can become the awareness of your existence and from this level of being, you are the most powerful. You can see exactly how you react to people, situations, and challenges.

The more you are able to do this, the more you realize you are not just this body and mind. This technique can be used in every aspect of your life—especially the places you struggle with.

36. Beliefs

Try to notice today in your own experience that we humans carry a lot of beliefs on pretty much every subject imaginable. We have gathered these notions throughout our upbringing and continue to gather more through the course of our lives. The thing is that some of these beliefs may be useful for you in this physical world, but only when you don't hold them like the ultimate truth.

Don't hold yourself back because you're stubborn and you are insisting that certain things are how you believe they are. Open your mind to the possibility that your beliefs are wrong and never engrave them so deeply in you that you're scared to change them.

Try to start noticing your beliefs through a third-person perspective, and really examine them anytime you can be aware of them. This can change the course of your life for the better as you start touching truth.

37. Voice in Your Head

Have you ever seen a person muttering to themselves about something? Well, we all do this, like it or not, and it might not be out loud. Try to take time today and be aware of the voice in your head, and really notice what it is saying to you.

Most people unfortunately, are so stuck in their mental stories that they can't even separate themselves for a second and just observe this happening. If you can start becoming the awareness of an experience, you then will be able to notice that your voice is a NUT Job and should be hospitalized! The really crazy part is that we believe what it says and then we get down on ourselves and feel unworthy.

Anytime you can have enough awareness to witness this happening, question this voice with some deep questions, instead of just believing it blindly.

38. Five Elements: Fire, Water, Air, Earth, and Space

Have you ever had an experience where you deeply noticed that everything, including you, is made out of some combination of these five elements?

There is a reason why you feel better when you really connect to even one of these elements on a deeper level. Why do you think you feel so good when you go to the beach, get into the wilderness, sit by a fire, breathe in clean air, stare into space? It's because you get a deeper connection to that part of you that is the same. Most people are too distracted by mind stuff to even have a connection like this consciously, but it's super powerful when you do.

Be aware of this anytime you come in contact with these elements, and try to really be grateful that you can experience these wonderful things.

39. Awakening

Many of the problems that you see occurring on our planet today are because we, as a species, were misguided into believing that happiness is brought about by external things. If you have such a notion, then of course you will be searching in the far depths of existence for this happiness, causing havoc as you go.

Awakening is the realization that nothing on this external world can bring about real happiness or joy; it's knowing that things are always temporary, and even if you gather a gazillion of them, they can only add to your happiness that you already experience within.

It is you understanding that you have the ability to connect to this inner joy at any given moment by removing yourself from your mind-created entity briefly and connecting to your fundamental nature.

Once you have awoken, you have temporarily separated from your fake entity and have touched your pure essence. The trouble is that the zombie will try to take over again and again because we live in a mind-dominated world—which means you have to put a conscious, dedicated effort into becoming more and more vigilant to spot the zombie.

40. Messenger

Be a messenger and help spread awareness to people around you. Do this by just being connected to your authentic self and showing people that they can be too. Have deeper conversations with people, by you becoming the space for them to be honest with you without your judgements and your ego's involvement.

Who are you to judge people anyway, as there are millions of ways to live, so why assume yours is the best?

It's okay if a person does something a different way than you; it's okay if somebody talks funny; it's okay if someone eats food differently than you; it's okay if somebody looks totally different than you. All these things are fine. Let the world be how it is, and let people be how they are.

Just start being you and let your message spread by your authenticity, not forcefulness.

41. Be Who You Are

Have you realized that you are totally different than other people? Yet you have been taught by society to try to fit in and be accepted. Start letting this go and try to be the real you in as many situations as you can today—preferably all of them.

Don't just try to please people or get scared of people's judgements. No matter how you are, they will judge—if they are disconnected from their true nature. Focus on yourself—notice anytime you aren't true and you are pretending. The more you notice this, the sooner you'll be able to start working on surrendering to your authentic self—because your awareness will expand and after a while, you'll get tired of being not you. It's a lot of work to be fake. Be real, be you always.

42. Time

Time is something that many people are confused about. Most people assume that time is so important. If you start working on yourself—as suggested by this book—one of the greatest realizations that you can experience is about time.

First, you will experience that time and your mind are connected. If you are not in your mind, time isn't real—because all you have is the present moment. *Now* is the only real time. Anything that ever happens or happened to you, was or comes in the present moment. Once it is not present, it is no longer a happening event—which is why it's so important to live in the present, rather than just trapped in thoughts in the mind.

Use time only for things that are necessary (like meeting people, going to work, and planning for things), but otherwise try to be in the present moment as frequently as possible. This way worry and anxiety will be much more minimal in your life. When you start feeling worried or anxious, use that as a sign that you've been taken out of the present and are stuck in time.

You cannot fight a dragon in the past or the future. You can only fight in the present moment. Don't fight things that aren't real. Allow them to come to the now and deal with them—because it doesn't make sense to fight something that might not even come.

43. Open-Minded

If you ask most people if they are open-minded, their answer will likely be yes. Is this true for them, and true for you?

After much investigation of this topic, I have realized that when people say that they are open-minded, they are answering from their mind-identified state, and usually their "yes" comes from a desire to not feel flawed—because society says open-mindedness is good. Usually they have not thoroughly investigated the question or the answer. If you start this experiment and are honest with yourself, you will quickly figure out that you and everybody else hold many beliefs that you feel are true, and those beliefs are then used to construct who you are. How can you then be open to the possibility of giving up many of those beliefs when your ego is created by them? Holding those beliefs is a matter of life and death for your ego!

Being open-minded means being able to use the things that come into our existence (both physical and mental) but then letting them go, for new things to come in without attachment, thus opening ourselves up for any possibility to exist at any moment.

You cannot be open fully when you make things that aren't you, you. If you do this, then you'll always need those things for your identity—yet they are not real; they are things you've just gathered.

44. Sensei: "person born before another" (Teacher)

It's important to surround yourself with people you can learn from. They don't have to have a big beard or live in a cave. They just need to be able to bring out your best in you, without forcing you, but by guiding you. Find your sensei or mentor. You will know such a person because you will feel loved (not flattered) in their presence. You will never have the sense that they need you in order to acquire something (importance as a teacher, etc.).

Make sure that you don't blindly believe what this or any person tells you. Question it, observe it, investigate it, look within, and test it with your inner guidance—your fundamental nature's wisdom.

Some people like to impart wisdom to you without actually experiencing it firsthand. That can be okay, but if you then make a belief out of it, you might have a bit of a problem—especially if the secondhand wisdom isn't beneficial to you—not all wisdom is helpful to all people. And secondhand wisdom is not always even the truth.

45. Be of Service to Others

The ego is all about me, but your true nature is about feeling the connection with existence, which is everything and everyone.

That being said, if you start going about your life by being of service to others, by using your skills in whatever way you love to, instead of trying to gain success by forcing it and making success your whole objective, you will see that not only is the universe going help you more often, but you will feel actual fulfillment, rather than just superficial success.

Unfortunately, a lot of people are run by their ego and they will do anything to be "successful," even if it means treating others and the world like garbage. Don't be like one of those people, because you might gain some money, but you definitely will not be successful or fulfilled.

46. Battle of Life

If you have lived long enough, you may have realized that life is a big journey to discovering who you really are. Unfortunately many people get stuck focusing on the negative aspects of their lives and never see what they have accomplished. It is important to try not to let your mind dwell on one event that didn't seem to go your way, and let it push you off your course.

Each and every one of us will go through many ups and downs in our lives, but you have to realize: that is the point. If you just lived in your comfort zone, you wouldn't experience life at all, because you'd be too scared to expand. Life gives you a kick in the butt sometimes to move you along. Yeah, it hurts for a little bit, but then you forget about it since the past fades away.

Most people seem to get stuck for a little bit when events turn out in a different way than they expected. Our expectations, though, are us believing our thoughts about how the future should turn out, and when it doesn't go as planned, our life seems to have gone off course. Don't let the couple of disappointments on your journey knock you down for long. You'll have learned more about yourself at the end of the disappointment than you would have known without it.

47. Duality

Everything on this outer world (physical) has an opposite: black/white, on/off, yes/no, success/failure, angry/happy, etc. If you have come to accept this through experience, then you will have noticed that whatever you have sought has resulted in you experiencing the opposite. Because everything has opposite sides, as there can't just be one without the other.

This is the nature of the physical world, but when you begin to look within and start touching your fundamental nature, there are no opposites. You can experience pure joy, peace, and love and you don't need to achieve anything to get it. You have to just let go of everything that is not you.

Try to notice that the spectrum that exists on the physical world is a blessing, not a curse. If there were not two sides, then you would not be able to see either good or evil, as you can only see things in comparison to other. The greatest lesson comes when you can merge the two forms into one, and realize that they go together and then there is no battle, as you have unity.

Leave the level of form at times to touch this nondual aspect of you; otherwise you will always be caught in the midst of the two of you, creating a battle with yourself.

48. Projection

Think of yourself as a projector, whatever goes on inside you is then reflected onto reality. When you perceive yourself and life in negative ways (such as hating yourself, feeling unworthy, lacking things, being a victim, etc.), these same qualities will be projected onto the physical world for you to experience.

The key is to notice when this happens and realize that you have been captured by your fake entity, and you are now manifesting these situations for yourself. Unfortunately instead of using this as a sign, most people get trapped in their mind-made stories and then blame those projections that they helped manifest on others and outer events.

For **example**, you think that the world is never fair and you always get robbed. If this is your mindset and feeling, then there is a much greater chance that this will become your reality, as this is what you are projecting and choosing to experience.

49. Downloading

Your body is an antenna, and luckily for you, it downloads information automatically. Right now you're downloading on basic mode, but if you take care of your body and learn to connect to it, it will become way more receptive for upgrades to come in.

Many people do not realize that we are multidimensional beings and are constantly downloading and receiving upgrades from all over the universe. We do live on a ball that is constantly moving and absorbing energies from all the other movement in space, so don't just assume that the only thing that affects you is things on earth.

The more you become aware that everything is connected and that you have the ability to receive information in all sorts of ways, the more in alignment you will be with life.

50. Bashing Others

Family gatherings, work-place chats, groups of friends, etc. are guaranteed to be filled with conversations that consist of putting other people down. Most humans are ruled by their ego, and one of its favorite ways to build itself up is to feel superior to others. Really unconscious people build up their self-esteem and self-worth this way.

When you are in a conversation today, try to step out and observe what you guys are talking about. If most of your conversations are how this person shouldn't do that, or my boss is an idiot, or why is that person dressing like that, and so on, then you're in a low state of consciousness and probably should start working on yourself a bit.

If you are aware of this happening, but your friends keep doing it, try not to feed their ego with ammunition because that's what egos seek. You are a perfect being already. It's the ego that is the fake entity of you and it constantly needs to be fed. Notice that this is the case and start starving the ego.

51. The Body

If you are like most people, first, you spend most of your life in your head, and second, you complain about your body a lot!

Instead of doing the "normal" thing, why not try to start using your body like the super-sophisticated technology that it is. If you can separate from your thinking for a moment, you will notice that your body is constantly telling you things, but you don't listen because you're too busy, lazy, or don't care about taking the time to learn what it tells you. **Example:** you eat something fake, it makes your stomach hurt, and instead of noticing that you shoved that thing in your mouth, you're thinking about how to make your stomach not hurt (usually artificially, aka pills), so you can eat more of that thing because everyone else seems to be doing it also, so it must be okay.

Tip:

Try to start feeling your body a couple of times a day—like really connecting to all the sensations in it—and don't let your mind come in and tell you that's a bad feeling and I have to get rid of it. Accept how you feel and allow it to be as it is, and see what you can learn from it. Obviously if your arm is dangling from its socket, then go get it fixed, but still accept that it happened.

When you start living in this way, you will be constantly open to learning, rather than exist as a chronic complainer.

52. Beautiful

How you see yourself on the outside is directly related to how connected you are to your true self internally.

Realize that your looks don't really change that much day to day; it's just your perception of yourself that changes. When you're fully connected to your truth, you feel and look beautiful no matter how your hair lies or whatever else usually bothers you. Now, when you're disconnected from your truth and you're stuck in your thoughts, that is when you start feeling inadequate. Changing your looks might give you temporary relief, but they will again haunt you, as this is a day-to-day scenario.

53. Be There Fully

A normal person's day consists of being captured by their mind. Some people believe they are thinking and they are somewhat in control, but if you examine this closer, you will notice that you are captured. To witness this, take a look at any activity or task that you perform today, and notice how much of your attention is actually there in that moment. If you are able to be aware for a second, then you will see that very minimal attention is given.

This happens in every aspect of your life: driving, eating, listening, working, etc.

Mostly, you spend time in your land of fiction. Try to start minimizing this throughout your day and make it a habit to have all your presence in the current moment.

If you keep doing this, you will be living most of your life in the realest moment and not in make-believe. The benefits are great, since a lot of the struggles you have are due to living in fakeness and hoping it will or won't come true.

54. Expanding Your Awareness

The greatest improvement you can make in your and other people's lives is through your expansion in awareness.

Most unconscious people see the world in a very ME-oriented awareness. They think that they are the center of it all, and everything is just happening to them. They see other people as ancillary players or competition to their success, and they see animals and all other creatures as things that exist for them as well. This is an **example** of having very little awareness.

As your awareness expands, you start being able to experience life in a bigger and clearer picture. You start noticing things like:

1. Every single person on this planet is exactly like you, dealing with their own struggles.

2. All animals and other beings value life just as much as you do.

3. Humans are a very miniscule part of the universe, and even though it sounds terrible, our lives don't mean too much.

4. The universe is constantly evolving by all its parts working as a collective.

5. Death and life are part of the same coin and one or the other isn't any better.

The more you start turning inward and letting intelligence shine through you, the higher in awareness you expand. Start to put some focus on gaining knowledge this way, instead of just picking up conceptual knowledge from others. Go straight to the source; it's were the truth lies, and the best part is that everyone has access to this.

55. Light Force

We all have an energy field around us, but the problem is that what we don't see, we don't believe.

Most people think they are their body and mind, but why is it some days you love yourself and think you're awesome and the next day you think you're ugly and terrible? It's not because you changed in one day, unless you're a chameleon. It's because you allow outer things to affect your energy field. If your energy field gets weakened, then you start believing you aren't worthy, or you're ugly, or whatever other fake issues that you decide to carry around.

Strengthen your energy field by connecting to it, and outer circumstances will never determine your well-being.

Tip:

Connect to your energy field by separating from your mind processes and being aware of your senses. Start feeling all the sensations that are going on inside and around you, and accept all of them fully, without labels, judgements, or conceptualizations from your mind. If you get stuck in a thought, let it be and just be aware that you got stuck, and get present again with all the sensations (good or bad). When you start doing this more and more frequently, you will start feeling a flow of energy through and around you.

56. Forgotten

Would it be crazy for you to understand that you have lived your whole life until this point in a very limited manner, not because you haven't achieved all your goals or become as successful as you've wished, but because you have forgotten something very crucial, and that is the understanding of who you really are.

This is the main reason it's easy for us to treat each other badly. When we have forgotten and think that we are just an individual, and not something more, we then view the world in a very limited way and at times feel that the world conspires against us, which makes us react in very unconscious ways.

For many people who are still trapped in the mainstream view, this is their primary way of living. They of course have great days, especially when outer things are going as they wish, but that doesn't last long. The majority of their days are spent in all types of distractions, but even then they have many low days and treat people and themselves in awful ways.

When you live from this unaware state, and barely ever touch the core of you, life will always be shallow and mostly about you and your needs. When you live connected to your fundamental self, amazing things start to happen in your life; you start seeing life and the connection you have with every single aspect of existence.

You can then oscillate between the two views, giving you a view from the physical and from the fundamental.

57. Strength

Have you noticed yet that true strength comes from being totally vulnerable and not needing to prove that you are strong? When you are able to be your full authentic self without being afraid of judgements, you then allow all your power to be released because you allow what is to be. This way you aren't subconsciously defending all the things that you are afraid of; you just accept them.

Bullies and people consumed by their ego, although they may seem strong and powerful on the outside, are actually the most weak. They constantly need to charge themselves by stealing other people's power. This is done by physical harm, emotional harm, and mental harm.

Try to be aware if you do this to others in any way, because then you're trying to gain strength from someone else's weaknesses and not just connecting to your truest and most powerful nature—which is the realization that you have always and will always be strong; you just need to tune in to it and let it come out of you.

58. Books

Have you ever realized that although reading books is an amazing thing to do to master stuff on this external world, it is also a very great way for your ego to build itself up? It seems like a lot of people on this planet gain tons of knowledge from reading, but all they really use that knowledge for is to recite it to others—not to help them, but to show how much more they know. This is what the ego does, as it is in competition with others and loves to feel superior.

Try to see if you do this as well. Do you secretly gain knowledge to better your life, or do you gain it to be "better" than others? Witness in your interactions if your ego is trying to compete on subjects with others, or if it can accept what others tell you, and your need to be better isn't in the forefront.

Also, witness that all knowledge is conceptual and not the truth of anything, which means that the more stuff you collect, idolize, and create beliefs of, the further you are from detaching from it and seeking truth from within.

59. Awakening through Music

Music can be such a powerful tool for you if utilized in a conscious manner. It can help you experience things outside of your mind if you allow it. To experience this, be conscious of how the sounds feel inside you and let the vibrations flow through your body without resisting.

Many people experience listening to music with just their mind, instead of letting it take them through their sensations, which is way more powerful. Rather than listening to whatever is most popular, try to choose music that raises your vibrations, and conscious artists who help uplift you. It will have a huge impact on your life.

Tip:

Your mood and emotions can be altered and affected by sounds, so be aware of what you are choosing to listen to. There is extensive research and capital invested in the music business, so try to realize that probably the most popular songs on the radio aren't really concerned with lifting your consciousness. Just because something sounds good or tastes good, doesn't mean it is good.

60. The Mind Is Abstract

I'm sure you have seen abstract artwork. It's usually done in paintings; it's the ones that look like a bunch of random stuff thrown together on a canvas to communicate something . . . or nothing, depending on the artist and the viewer. This is how your mind operates as well. It gathers a bunch of information and then tries to form a picture with it that either tells you what a thing is, as accurately as possible, or obscures it because it might be threatening.

This might not seem like a big deal, but think of everything you see in your day-to-day life, moment by moment. Each time you look at something, you only see a tiny snippet of what is actually there.

As kids, teenagers, or even as adults we may wish we were living another person's life, such as a celebrity's, based on the snippets of what we see. The thing is that you see maybe five percent of their life, and you then believe their life is glamorous in most areas and something you would prefer.

Or when you look at other people, your mind automatically just sees their appearance, style, skin color, and thinks it knows much about them, because it compares them to all the propaganda you have gathered about those things in the past, as if it's the ultimate truth for everything.

Make sure you really are conscious with your snippet gathering. The next time you think that you know everything, try to remember that you actually can't; it is in fact impossible to know everything through the way of the mind. You need to get past the mind or you will always live in a fragmented reality. Start perceiving things through your senses and observing things without your mind telling you what they are.

61. Friends

The word "friend" is used in many contexts and means different things to different people. When a person is operating primarily out of their mind-identified state, no matter how good of a friend someone is to you, they are still just an entity that your ego uses for comparing, judging, analyzing and competing against.

The more your awareness expands, the more you realize that the friendships that you currently have are mostly very low-conscious, and they are almost always just connected on the level of the mind. There are exceptions of course, especially if you grow up with someone, or connect on a deeper level with them, but even then, anytime your Zombie Mode kicks in, that friendship can end pretty quickly due to outer circumstances.

It is important to realize that we were tricked when growing up with today's technology—the more friends we have, the better, we think. Understand that most of the people you've added on Facebook and other social networks are not high-quality friendships, but are either a result of your competitive nature or are people you've met a couple of times and have never truly connected with.

When examining your friendships, try to ask yourself these questions:

Are you able to be fully you with your friends? Not needing to pretend to like what they like, go places where you don't really want to go, and do things you don't want to do?

Are you able to accept your friends no matter what they do or who they are? Can they do the same for you?

Tip:

Make sure you try to become the space for your friends to be themselves. It's an amazingly powerful way to help someone. Try to get out of your mind when you are in a conversation with your friends and try to listen with all of your senses. Don't judge or compete; just be there. Notice how your energy is with them and the sensations you feel inside your body anytime you interact. This will give you a powerful experience and an amazing connection.

62. Family

If you ask people what matters most, one of the most dominant answers is family, unless you grew up without a real family or in a very dysfunctional one. The important thing to notice here is that even though you spent most of your life with these people and have seen a lot of the same things as your siblings and parents, all of you still carry all types of different beliefs and ideologies about life.

Now just because you get into disagreements and fights over these beliefs, most of you probably wouldn't kill each other, right? (Although that does happen in our world.)

The point is that your beliefs and ideologies will always be questioned and disagreed with by many people, because that's how reality works. The biggest lesson from this is that you need to be able to separate yourself from those things that you carry so firmly, because your ego considers them to be you—this is why you defend them so fiercely.

Start practicing letting go of your false self (all things picked up) especially when you disagree with a family member. This doesn't mean you have to think that what they say is right. Just don't let something consume your inner peace. Don't fight egos. It's a lose, lose practice. Once you can do this with family and friends, you can then start doing it with everyone else.

63. Routine

A process that is so engrained into your mind that it becomes almost automatic.

Try to be aware today of your routines, as it is very easy to get so programmed into doing certain things a certain way that you're not aware that you act in that manner anymore.

Routines have benefits but they can also cause you to get stuck in certain patterns, which aren't beneficial to your growth and restrict you from living the life that you want. This happens in eating, social gatherings, driving, parenting, working, learning, etc.

Try to notice this for yourself by noticing it in a direct experience of your friend, your partner, or a family member who is living their routine. It is much easier for you to see this in someone else and wonder why they are doing that. Try not to judge them; just observe and notice how they aren't really aware of what they're doing; they're just doing it. Now see that you are doing this too, and the problem is that you don't see it either, because you are either stuck in the future or the past. You're caught up in all types of mind

stories and aren't noticing that your routine
is no longer serving you.

64. Labeled

The more labels you collect about you, the
further you get from your true self. If you
stop identifying yourself based upon the labels
that you and society have put on you, the less
suffering you're going to have in your life.
This is because you won't feel the need to try
to defend your fake self if someone or some
situation questions one of those labels—which
aren't even you.

For **example**, if one of your labels is
that you think you're pretty, but then someone
says you're ugly, you will get defensive and
angry, and it will cause you pain. But if you
think about it, nothing really changed. That
person telling you that you are ugly has
nothing to do with you or how you look.
Obviously that person has some problems and is
trying to get a lift in energy by taking yours.

You are already a perfect being from the
start. You just happened to collect some Post-
it® notes with words describing you, and now
anytime a person or situation contradicts your
Post-it note, you react because you think that
Post-it note you collected is the ultimate
truth of you, but it's not.

You are beyond any label.

65. Avatar

Here is a little perspective switch that you can play around with—when you see a person walking by you, or when you're with a friend, or at work—imagine that the physical body of the other people are just avatars and that something more fundamental is inhabiting those avatars.

The mind really gets hung up on the avatar (outer shell) itself and the actions done by it, but today just try and focus on this other view. Connect the being inside your physical shell with theirs by not identifying with all your mind activity, such as; the labels, the judgments, or any other additions it tries to impose on them.

Once you can touch what you are fundamentally yourself, it will be easier to see others in that same way. If you're always just living from your mind entity, then these types of perspective switches will not be possible.

Don't just assume that your current perspective is the most valid one, practice using different perspectives and see what can be discovered.

66. Forgiveness

An action that many people can't seem to perform when they are being operated by their ego. When you can connect to your fundamental nature, outside of your mind-created self, you can truly forgive people.

Most people, including me of course, have a super hard time forgiving when we are run by our ego. Many of us say we forgive, but our ego makes us feel bitter, and we have some hate toward others.

This is because your ego thinks that other people took something away from you, hurt you in some way or the people that you care about, and since you have never stepped outside of your mind-identified state, that's all you know, and of course it's going to cause you pain.

You can actually learn to get outside of your ego and connect to your truest nature, more and more often, and realize that everyone in their core is pure existence, and whatever they might have or might not have done, it's not who they really are on the most fundamental level. Therefore if you cannot forgive others, it's because you're still consumed on some level by your mind, and by not forgiving your mind thinks it's keeping power, which is actually the opposite of the truth.

67. Enemy

A person who your mind believes is a threat, due to past events, future projections, or conditioning. Witness in yourself that as long as you have enemies, you are consumed by your mind-identified self.

Yes, it's a fact that people are unconscious and they do a lot of stupid things to others, the world, and especially themselves. But there is no need to create enemies out of these people, because, if you do, you're sinking back into unconsciousness yourself—which your zombie mind loves. Work on dissolving the need to create enemies out of people, as this is one of the ways we are destroying ourselves.

When unconscious people enter your life, you can still take action when you need to, but please realize that they are just an unconscious being who is walking around like a zombie, oblivious to the harm that they are doing.

The best way to fight these people is with your consciousness—by being so conscious that whatever they throw at you gets extinguished and their unconsciousness gets transmuted into brief moments of consciousness.

Sometimes it is necessary to stop these people in more aggressive ways, but even then,

you do it in a conscious manner, and not
through mind-identified means.

68. Existence

Try to notice today that the whole point of
your life is to experience existence.

We get so caught up with our success and
failures and all the other distractions on this
physical world that we don't see that there is
nothing that we have to be doing other than
experiencing this existence in whatever way we
choose. Obviously there are many things out of
your control, but you have to allow those to
be.

The ego covers this up and, since most of
the time people are run by their minds, they
can't get back to this realization of just
being. They try to achieve, gather, and become
all sorts of things, as they believe that
success in life is measured by what you have
and the legacy you can leave behind.

Start shifting your awareness to
experiencing existence in the way it comes to
you. Make decisions, then accept them and what
comes with them. The more you are able to
accept existence, the more enjoyable a life you
will live.

69. Fairy Tales

Have you ever witnessed that you live a lot of your life in fiction? Stories of all kinds have been told to you as a child about distant lands, dragons, princesses, and all sorts of magical creatures, and you know not to believe those, yet the stories that your mind tells you in day-to-day life you believe—mostly without question.

If you observe yourself on a daily basis, you will notice that your mind is constantly creating fairy tales and horror stories about reality, by adding to it props, characters, and all types of scenarios. It's really cool that we as human's have this ability to envision things, but over time your mind tricks you and keeps you in fantasy longer, even adding emotions to the story, which makes for compelling realism.

In tough times especially, the mind keeps you stuck thinking about a break-up, death, disease, etc. Some people can never live in reality once they've experienced something tough. Often you see this in scenarios of loss; people get captured in their emotions and think about how dreadful the future will be without whatever they lost, or they constantly play back the past to try to feel better.

It's nice to be able to float around and imagine, but always get back to the present moment as often as you can. If you do this, it will start slowing down the momentum of thoughts and emotions, and eventually you will start feeling peace.

70. Obstacles/Challenges/Problems

In every person's life, there are many moments of what seems like unfavorable circumstances. In reality, something just happens—but in one's mind, it is us getting treated unfairly by life.

During this time, it is super important to notice your internal condition. The problem is that during so-called unfair circumstances, the mind comes in full force and unconsciousness rules, causing you to switch into Zombie Mode. You then start operating from your programmed self, while you play the victim game in your head.

The key thing is to evoke your peacefulness.

For **example**, you are on the way to the airport, and there is major traffic, leaving you only a small margin of time to catch your flight. Automatically your internal condition will have moved from peaceful to racing with anxiety, because your mind has taken over and is supplying you with enough thoughts to shoot a full soap opera episode. Now with your internal state taken over, your external reality becomes chaotic. You're rushing, angry, panicky, and guess how good that is for your internal health? Not to mention you're operating your super sophisticated human vehicle, like a person trying to learn how to drive stick shift for the first time.

Try to start being aware of your inner condition when things don't go your way. If you just focus your awareness on this area of your life, seeing the gap between reality (a mere traffic jam, a schedule problem) and your mind game (life vs. death), you can experience tremendous growth.

71. Game of Life

Have you ever noticed that life is like a game? The biggest problem is that you have not read the instructions for how to use this character you are playing, so instead of it being fun and enjoyable, the game has become frustrating and confusing.

Pause for a second and start realizing that you aren't trapped anywhere, and every time you get stuck, you have the choice to get up and head back in the right direction.

It is also important to remember that there is no right or wrong way to play the game, but be willing to accept the circumstances that come up based on the moves that you decided to make either consciously or unconsciously.

Tip:

Life will be a much more enjoyable experience when you actually start looking within you for the answers instead of asking others to supply your controls. Master yourself. Master the game.

72. Re-Program

As we develop into fully capable human beings, many programs get downloaded onto us, mostly out of our control as we are still learning life's normal customs. These programs come from your parents, friends, teachers, books, TV, movies, and anywhere else you have contact. Some of the people who program you are trying to do the best they can for you; they seek to protect you, but at the same time they are limiting you.

You are perfectly capable of learning through all your senses, but humans are so quick to rush you into learning all the rules of life that they have learned and try to help you avoid the mistakes they have made. The problem is that all those well-meaning programs are acquired through their conceptualized and distorted view.

Since you can't go back in time, focus on the now and start RE-PROGRAMMING what no longer is beneficial to your growth.

Try to be aware of the operating programs as you function; be conscious of anything that is limiting you from your full potential. When you can witness yourself operating in situations through a program, you might feel unworthy, disconnected, fearful, judgmental, etc. Notice it and, as often as possible, be fully present when it is happening. If you are able to see that unconscious programs are directing your actions, this alone is a huge step toward changing your condition.

Tip:

Notice how you act toward people, the words you use when you are in conversations, the activities that you engage in and are willing to try, the things you are scared of, and other things of this nature. These are all clues that can help you realize what programs are running you.

73. Pets

The acts of barking, meowing, and hissing are all natural ways that some animals express themselves. Yet humans have all sorts of ways of relating to this communication. Seeing how you act with your pets can lead to a consciousness shift. Try to be aware in your own experience when your dog barks—how your state of consciousness changes when your pet does something you don't think it should.

Many people snap into an unconscious state and get upset, hit their pet, yell at them, or worse.

Realize that you are just having an experience of having a pet. Animals are their own beings with their own reasons for reacting as they do. It's only humans who think they can or should control everything. Why don't your pets and kids do what you want them to do all the time? It's because living beings aren't robots; they flow with life in their own ways, just like you do in yours.

Always remember that you are experiencing this life with all its aspects—including other beings with different needs and reactions from your own—and allow things to be and learn to accept things instead of letting them change your inner state. Yes, your mind tells you that it shouldn't be like that, but—news flash—it should be how it is, as that is what *is*.

74. Confidence

Did you know that many people struggle mightily with confidence? I would be willing to bet that you do as well in some areas of your life. This is mostly due to the way you and others derive their confidence, and that is by competing and trying to be better than others.

Instead of gaining confidence in this manner, which is very temporary and egoic, try to start realizing that you don't need to be better and compete with others in order to build confidence, as at your core you are fully confident already, and this always exists at every moment for you.

You need to just touch this within you by separating from your mind, as that is what makes you feel not confident. The mind does this by running scenarios from your past and even showing you glimpses of the future if you don't win or if you mess up. Stop giving so much power to your mind. It's just a tool to help you in this life, yet you allow it to bully you, and when you get fed up with being bullied, you bully others to feel better about yourself.

The mind has created a fake you by storing experiences that have passed and then playing them back for you. They are just experiences that you once had at an earlier stage of your awareness. You are in a different stage now, so those moments that the mind plays can't be you. You are always in the present moment, and after that passes, it's not you anymore. You again are in the present moment, so live there.

75. Empathy

Are you able to tap into this ability in you yet?

We are all connected beings in this world. That is no secret, but unfortunately most people are so consumed by themselves (ego) that they never feel this or, if they do, their mind makes it into a problem.

If you start connecting to your inner self and feeling the sensations going on inside you, outside of your mind's control, you will notice that others have an impact on those sensations.

Start separating from your mind-made self and live with some attention in your inner being, so that you can be vigilant about how other people can affect you.

This can help you connect with others in ways that are more powerful than just with the mind.

76. Be a Rebel

Break the rules if they don't apply. If you're doing this consciously, you are not causing harm, and you're raising your awareness.

Did you know that rules were made by people? And people operate at different levels of consciousness—some closer to zombies than humans. Therefore some rules might not be serving you anymore, and if they are stopping you from evolving, then maybe it's okay to break them.

You're not a robot, you know? Your own inner intelligence knows what is right and wrong. You don't need a rule to tell you that. The problem is that you have been taught from early on that if you don't follow rules, you will be punished, and now you're scared of everything, and you believe rules are the truth.

Rules are great for unconscious humans, but if you are conscious, you have no desire to hurt or do harm to others or the planet. Get fully conscious, so that you don't need rules to function in life, and use your common sense.

77. Space/Thing Consciousness

What is space? Have you ever thought about this?

Nobody pays much attention to space, and I'm not just talking about outer space, but space in the sense of nothing. Realize that most of your attention is always taken up by things, including mind activities (thoughts and emotions).

You might be thinking, Okay, why would I even pay attention to space (nothing)? Well,

have you noticed that space exists everywhere?
Even inside you, inside your cells, and in
everything else?

If that's the case, then have you ever
wondered if space might be important since it's
one of the constants in everything?

If you take time to contemplate this, you
will realize that space is super important
because without it, nothing would be able to
exist. If you look even deeper, you will also
realize that you have the ability to connect to
this space, which is one of the most amazing
and powerful experiences that you can ever come
across.

If you can get out of your mind and
separate from thing consciousness, you can
touch the space that exists not only inside you
but all over existence. When you do this, you
become connected to everything, as space is
everywhere and the peace and aliveness that you
feel when you touch this space
(Nothing)(Emptiness)(Silence)(Stillness) is
unexplainable.

78. Revenge

Why is revenge just an egoic way of trying to
gain back false power? When you execute your
revenge tactics on the person or persons who
hurt you, sure, your mind will tell you that
you got even, but as you probably have noticed,

your mind is a liar a lot of the time, and that is definitely the case here.

The reason revenge never works out is because the person who you seek vengeance on is unconscious, otherwise they would not have done what they have done, and now you decide to turn unconscious to do a similar act.

If you are fully conscious, you are connected with everyone and you realize, no matter how idiotic a person may act, they are still the same thing as you, and therefore you sinking to unconsciousness again just doesn't make sense.

If you want growth and self-mastery, you have to be able to accept that many people in this world are still very unconscious and if you act like an asshole to others based on what others do to you, then we'll continue to have the same type of world that we are living in today—a world filled with zombies, acting like assholes to not only humans, but to all types of living creatures.

Also, you have to notice that you seek revenge because you feel like someone has taken something from you or hurt you, but that is just what your mind-made self makes you believe. Nobody can take anything away from you ever. Yes, they can take physical objects, but those are all just attachments and not really yours anyway.

79. Throw Out the Trash

Picture this: You have a room, and in this room you only have a certain amount of space. It's a decent size room, but there is some stuff already in it—the most important things that come with the room and need to be there.

Now throughout your life, you constantly collect more things and just shove them in this room, without really organizing or being vigilant about the fact that there is only a certain amount of space. As you grow, this is normal because you don't really know what will be useful, so you grab anything you can find and throw it in.

After many years though, this room has become so full, that you can barely shut the door. Things are falling and breaking, and you can't even get to some of the things you collected, because not only are you not aware that they are there, but it's impossible to get to them with everything else in the way.

Most people go their whole lives collecting and adding things to this room, NEVER taking time to throw out and organize things in such a way that you can get to every area easily.

Basically what I am tell you is OPEN THE DAMN DOOR and start throwing stuff out! It's a process and it will be tough at times, but if you don't do this, you will never know which things are the ones that came with the room and are FUNDAMENTAL.

80. Food and Consciousness Linked

Have you ever noticed that the foods that you choose to eat are directly linked to how conscious you are when you eat?

When you are highly conscious, you are connected to life, and typically you will eat more healthy foods as the vibration of your frequency matches those foods.

Unfortunately society in general is super low conscious, and you can see this by the foods that are popular with the majority. As a collective, we struggle with ourselves so greatly that foods have become a means to cheer us up. I am not saying you can't enjoy food, but when a food is poisoning your body so much that you need to take pills to feel better, that might be a sign to stop, don't you think?

Try to start taking time to be aware of the food that you choose to eat. Really notice how you're feeling internally as you're choosing the food, while you're eating it, and after you have consumed it. Put your attention on the sensations in your body, your thoughts and feelings, and just observe.

The more you work on consciousness, self-mastery, and meditation, the less you will be inclined to fuel yourself with pollution, aka terrible food.

Many people have become so unaware of the sensations in their bodies that they don't even notice that food is a big deal and makes them feel a certain way, since feeling shitty is just normal for them.

Work on yourself and start questioning the choices you make on food, because eating things just because others are doing it shouldn't be your main directing principle.

81. Fear Be Gone

I spoke briefly about fear in the beginning of the book (spiders), but I will explain this in a bit more detail here, as fear is one of the main ways that the mind keeps us trapped.

The main thing you need to understand about fear is that it is a mind tactic used to deter you from trying new things or to keep you from doing things that you have done in the past, which resulted in a "bad" experience(s).

Our mind is basically a computer and it stores all sorts of information (data) for us, which it then uses to evaluate new experiences (great tool). The problem is that when you experience an event that is similar to something you did in the past, your mind automatically brings back that stored data in thoughts and emotions and keeps playing it for you as long as your attention is consumed by your mind. It also uses past data to project future possible outcomes if you experience this event (and since there are millions of possibilities, this is basically fiction).

The key to dissolving any fear is to get totally present in the now and stay there while you experience the fearful event and afterwards as well. When we are about to experience something scary, our mind takes over our attention and keeps us trapped while it plays all types of scenarios that may occur. If you can realize that every experience is its own experience, then you will be able to use past data as a guide, but take that new experience fully connected to the present moment, which is how you can step away from the mind and regain your control.

It is the mind that keeps us scared, not the actual event. Learn to separate from your mind and this will help you conquer your fears a lot easier.

82. How Many Days?

Have you ever asked yourself how many days you were actually joyous for life? Like really try to take some time and think back on your last month maybe, and try to see how many of those days you went to sleep full of joy.

Unfortunately, for most people, this is a very low number and instead of having joyous days and loving life, they are annoyed, frustrated, angry, and feel like the world is treating them unfairly. If this is how you feel, then that is okay. Just accept that is how you feel, but then also notice that you are letting outer events dictate your happiness and joy. That is like saying, only if it is sunny I will be happy. What happens on those other days? You can't be happy?

If you start looking within yourself and investigating this at the core, you will notice that your mind-identified state creates many limitations for your joy and happiness because it sets perimeters on what needs to happen for you to feel that. Start working on dis-identifying with your mind-made self and touching your true nature to make the number of days of joy and happiness to skyrocket—nothing needs to happen on the outer world for your true nature to love life, as existing is the joy of life.

If you stop taking existing for granted, you might be able to realize that existing is one kick-ass miracle, yet most people don't care about it, as they live trapped in their mind. But as far as the mind is concerned, even if you had a pet dragon, a swimming pool full of cash, 200 cars, mansions in each country, a plane, a rocket ship, a yacht, and whatever else floats your boat, you still would need more to sustain your mind-made happiness.

Have you noticed that a kid can play with a twig and be happy, a cat is fully satisfied with a string, and a dog sometimes just needs his or her own tail? An adult on the other hand . . .

83. Coffee

The magical dark substance that has the power to make an adult's day go from terrible to better.

Nope, I didn't realize that coffee is the greatest thing on the planet. I realized how powerful of a program coffee can be.

Obviously if you don't drink coffee, then take something else that you need to have daily and see its power over you. I'm not trying to tell you not to drink or like coffee, as nobody should be telling you what to do. I'm just trying to show you how much power such a thing as coffee can possess.

Try to do an experiment today on yourself by making a decision not to drink coffee for one day and notice the resistance your mind puts up and how it puts you in all types of moods by telling you things such as: If I don't drink coffee I will be tired, if I don't drink coffee I will be miserable, if I don't drink coffee I won't have a good day, etc. The question is, is this actually true?

The whole point of this is to realize how much power we give to certain things over us. This is just coffee, but there are so many areas in your life where you are held back because the power of your mind over you is too great to shake.

If you want growth in your life, try to test yourself at times by doing simple things such as this to break the hold that certain things have on you.

Tip:

You can do this with sleep, with food, with a route you take to work, or any area where your mind makes you believe that if you change that routine it will not be good. Remember that the outer world is temporary and things change all the time, so the more you can change without too much attachment, the less suffering you will have in your life.

84. Flexibility

In order to suffer the least amount on this physical world, you need to be able to work on becoming flexible. By becoming flexible I mean both with your body and in events, with people, in circumstances, etc.

When you start working on becoming flexible through working with your body (yoga), you not only start feeling better physically, but you start becoming more aware of how you have been rigid in the other parts of your life.

When you start learning to become more flexible in all areas of your life, you will notice that you can let things be how they are more often without needing them to be a certain way, and that is a powerful way to approach challenging situations.

If you haven't noticed yet, reality is very unpredictable and when you aren't able to be flexible, you will try to fight reality, which, in my own experience, never works out too great. Think of water, as it were a great teacher of flexibility. Consider that its flexibility might be the reason it is the most powerful and abundant substance on the planet.

85. Centipede

It is perfectly acceptable that humans are scared of whatever they do not know. Since this is the case we try to destroy everything that is different, as that seems to be the easiest solution, especially when we are in the position of power and run by the mind.

Think of this **example**:

If a human was to see a centipede in their house, usually the typical unconscious response would take place and DESTROYING the enemy is what would happen. The enemy is obviously not even an enemy; it's just that most humans are scared unconscious ignorant zombies using their bigger avatar vehicles to destroy anything that doesn't fit in their minds ideal conceptualized version of reality.

Now let's take this on a different level... Since most humans are unconscious and do this to a little bug that's mostly harmless, what they do to other humans that are different from them is much the same.

An idiot could understand that if you live on different parts of the earth, the way you will look and act will be totally different than another human from a different part of the earth, Right?

When something is different, weird, strange, unique, it doesn't mean it's a threat. It actually means expansion if one would just open their mind. You take in something new from actual reality and get to expand the model of your conceptualized version of reality that you were living from through the mind. This means you grow, you expand your bubble.

People who are deeply unconscious aren't allowed to expand because their mind makes them afraid (fear is the minds security system) the mind uses it to protect the small little bubble of what it has convinced you that reality actually is and should be, and that's how your living life.

Don't be a zombie, start being human by just prying open your mind just a little bit, because your mind's version of reality isn't true, it's very distorted. When you're stuck in it though, it feels and seems very truthful, this is a lie and needs to be seen through direct experience and outside of it.

86. Compassion

Try to notice today in your own experience that when you start operating more frequently in the mode of compassion, you start allowing more energies to come into you, instead of shielding yourself and being scared to let anything in.

When you make it a habit to operate through compassion, you tell the universe that you understand that there is a greater force in play, instead of you being a scrooge and only thinking that you matter.

Obviously, you still need to make sure that you value you, but at least at times, separate from your ME mode and put your awareness onto having compassion for the world.

The collective is much more powerful than just you, as the collective is a ton of you's all together in one. Imagine Godzilla were real and you were fighting him alone. Now think of you and thousands of other you's versus Godzilla. Way better odds, right?

Compassion is like the joining of forces with universe. Don't be a dumbass; it just makes sense.

87. Weaknesses

Have you ever examined what weaknesses are? Weaknesses are your mind-created label for what you didn't do as well as another person, based on society's rules.

Really, please look into this on a deep level because it can help you suffer a lot less on the level of the physical world.

On the outer world, we are capable of using our bodies and mind in many amazing ways. Some people can do this or that better than you, while you can do this or that better than them. Comparing abilities is a cool little game that we all can play, but the key is to not get so caught up in this game, because for many people it eventually starts determining their worth.

Of course you can play this game and try to improve certain areas of your life, but continue to remind yourself that your capabilities with this physical body aren't a very important factor in the totality of life.

Also, notice that if you feel like you are weaker in a particular area of your life, then use that sign and put some effort into improving it if it will help you grow as a human being and expand your awareness. If it's just to be better than other people, you can play that game too, but understand that at some point it will cause you to suffer, as the ego is in control of your life.

88. Mystical

Just because you can't understand things logically doesn't mean they can't be real. The mind is limited and if you base everything on your mind, you will be limited in your experience. Remember how people used to think that the world was flat? Well, basically we are no different today. Just because we can see more doesn't mean that we aren't as ignorant as the people who were convinced that the world was flat and refused to think otherwise. When one is run by the ego, one thinks one knows everything; when one is open to all possibilities, one can be open to understanding beyond the physical limits.

If you sit down and really take a look at life, you will quickly realize that you don't understand anything. Do you know how you breathe? How you are able to see things? How you walk? How you hear? Maybe you know bits and pieces of very minor information about those areas, but in reality you don't know much.

Step outside of your mind at times and tune inward to understand other realms.

89. Comfort

Have you ever built a box and lived in it? Well, this is primarily what you are doing when you are searching for comfort. It is nice to have some level of comfort in life, but ultimately comfort is a trap. It is disguised as a great thing and many people seek it, but if you really investigate this, you will notice that comfort leads to fear. When you get comfortable, you are staying still and not growing and changing.

If you look at the world through a larger lens, the only thing that is constant is change, and we as humans unfortunately have been conditioned into thinking that when this happens or that happens, then we will be set.

This is an illusion and you have to try to snap out of it anytime you get too comfortable in an area of your life, because it too will change without you noticing it and then you will suffer a lot.

Start searching in your life for areas that you are comfortable in and try to shake that comfort up by doing something different or at least viewing the area from a different perspective.

Why do you think we age? And go through different stages of life? It's so that we keep experiencing new things and not just living in comfort. Start getting comfortable being uncomfortable because, either way, your comfort will not last long, and it's going to keep you stuck.

90. Science

There is no doubt that science has brought us many amazing discoveries and will continue, but nevertheless, it is a mental creation and as such will never be able to see beyond that. It is limited.

Science dissects things and makes assumptions, it will not find the fundamental truth as that is beyond itself (beyond the mind). Just as you knowing where I'm from will not tell you who I am, the most it will ever give is snippets about my physical life. The same way science will not be able to find out who I am by dissecting me and putting me back together. I am beyond the mind and body and so are you.

What we are fundamentally is beyond science, so if you're hoping that one day all will be explained about life through it, your living in an illusion. Science plays in the realm of the physical, and you are not just physical.

Notice that humans created science. Science didn't create us. It's trying to recreate us and all other beings because the mind needs to know, yet it cannot because it's the blockage point. One must travel beyond the mind to reach pure truth and that's the secret that most super smart people can't grasp because they are so involved in their mind, it sounds like absurdity for them to go beyond it.

If you want to be smart continue in the realm of the mental, if you want to be intelligent and know beyond the physical, beyond limits, then you must go beyond the mind, beyond science.

You can't drive a car in the air, it's good for the road, but you need something different to fly.

91. Saying No

This might not seem like a big deal to some people, but there are many others who have a really hard time saying no. Try to be aware today in your own experience if you have trouble saying no—whether it's to friends, family members, coworkers, etc.

If you can relate to this, then you have to understand that what you are doing in your life is just as important as another person, and when a road block comes, such as people that you no longer resonate with, or experiences that you choose not to have anymore, then it's okay to say no. This doesn't have to be a monumental event; if someone asks you to go somewhere and you don't want to, don't think that you have to because they put some pressure on you. Many people are very egoic and they try to push others around as that feeds their ego, and some people have a hard time saying no.

When I started to really work on myself and made dramatic changes in what I ate, who I hung out with, what I chose to do with my time, some people did not understand what I was doing and sometimes they tried to make a big deal about it. This is all okay too; they don't have to understand or even support you. The most important thing is that you have to value you, because if you don't, then you'll just be a puppet of society, following what it tells you to do.

Say no even if it means a harder journey or fewer friends. Your true self is always worth it.

92. Words

Have you ever noticed that words are basically organized sounds that humans create to help express and reflect back vibrations? All sounds are frequencies that oscillate at certain speeds, creating a certain vibration through you and the world.

Try to really comprehend this on a deep level, as words then are very powerful tools that we can use to create and reflect back vibrations. If you ever have looked into vibrations deeply, you have probably found that vibrations are super important as they can change your experience of life.

Since most people aren't really conscious in general, when they communicate with others and with themselves, they use words that express and reflect back low conscious vibrations, leaving them to experience only the same.

When you start noticing the words that you are using, you will see that there are patterns that show up, and those patterns are your programs that are operating you.

You can see this first by observing your conversations with family or friends. When you talk with them, really be aware of what they say as a response to certain things. If you do this, you will see that people tend to say the same words quite often, and respond based on the programs that are running them.

For **example**, notice that some people always reject new ideas or plans that people have, or some people always use words that blame the world, or they are very unsure of things they say, etc.

All these are clues that you can look for to find your programs in you. Be aware today of every response that you make and question them. Words are vibrations, so be aware which vibrations you'd like to come back to you.

93. Stillness

Try to notice today in your own experience that we have a really hard time being still, and even if we have the opportunity to be still, we feel uncomfortable and prefer to distract ourselves by entertainment or other means.

The problem with this is that you can't ever feel at peace this way, as you are trapped in your mind, which is linked with time. If you can make an effort and work on becoming still internally, the same will start being reflected for you outwardly.

If you touch stillness in your life, you will notice that it brings the most upmost peace that you can feel. Stillness is like you stop time and just start existing in the current moment, which is where your essence always exists. Unfortunately for most people, this way of being will never be touched, yet it is the most amazing way of living life.

The beauty about stillness is that it is where your most fundamental nature resides. It is your mind-made self that is always stuck in time. Don't get lost in time; be still and live in peace.

94. Mantras

Our mind can feed us large amounts of negativity due to all types of scenarios. If you can step away and notice that it is happening to you, it is very beneficial to use a mantra to help break out of your mind's hold.

If you aren't familiar with what a mantra is, it is basically just a saying or a phrase that you repeat to yourself in order to start vibrating on a higher frequency.

You can use all types of mantras based on your needs in a particular moment. For **example**, if you're struggling with finding love, you can say something like, I am worthy and open to receive an abundance of love in my life. You can obviously make up your own mantra as well.

Just make sure that you commit to it, because if you say something once or twice and then start getting again caught up in your mind's stories about how you're a victim and this isn't possible for you, then the mantra won't help much.

Try this out today and notice the shift
of energy that happens for you when you can
truly separate from your mind's negativity.

95. Healing

The super power that humans actually do have,
yet we are too busy to notice as our mind
distracts us with useless things or makes us
believe it's not really that big a deal.

What is more miraculous than us having
this super power is that you don't need to do
much for healing to occur, yet even with
healing we sabotage ourselves.

Most people can't disconnect from their
mind processes in general, but when they have
become sick or injured, it is nonstop; instead
of helping their body heal itself by being
fully connected to all its essence, they are
consumed by the mental aspect of the problem.

If action is needed because your leg is
dangling from its socket, then take the
necessary steps to help, but if the helping
that you are doing is you being consumed by
your mind's fictitious stories about the event
or the future, then basically you are just
taken over—in Zombie Mode—and you are using
vital energy to power the mind's sabotage.

If your body is at ease, it is going to
heal itself in a way more efficient manner than

if you're constantly in a victim mentality. Start realizing that you're not doing yourself and your body any good by constantly using up energy to fantasize all the possibilities that can occur.

Think of yourself as a phone with a battery; the more you're doing stuff with it, the more your battery drains. Healing takes a lot of battery life, but instead of allowing it most of the battery, you decide to give the mind a good chunk, and not only does it take a lot of battery life, but very often it counteracts your healing by adding its own extra shenanigans.

Your job is to allow healing to occur and surrender to it, not control it.

96. Rushing

Have you been able to notice in your own life that you are always being rushed and it's mostly caused by your own mind?

Observe how you operate in your day, and you will see that you are being rushed as long as you are consumed by your mind, which for most people is most of the time. Your mind is connected with time, and the more that it's active, the more rushed you are going to feel (anxiety).

Are you rushing to achieve something? If you are, then try to stop for a second and ask yourself if the rushing part is necessary to this scenario.

If you take a look inward, you will be able to admit that the rushing part is just a mind tactic making you believe that when you rush to something and get it, then you will be happy, fulfilled, satisfied, but has that ever happened for real? Or were you again rushing after you got that thing to get to the next thing?

Check for yourself, unless you want to continue to rush through your life in search of happiness. Work toward your goals but enjoy each part of the journey.

97. Turtle (Value of Slowing Down)

In our society, we humans are taught that being quick and strong is always the better option. We idolize animals such as a cheetah or lion—which is great, as they are amazing animals—but try to take a different perspective today and be more like a turtle, as the faster you operate, the less you can soak in an experience.

You can cover more ground by being fast, but when you move at a slower speed like a turtle, you can really be aware of a lot more of an area, as you spend more time in it.

Try to be a turtle today in your life, and really take time to notice as much as you possibly can by not rushing anywhere, but by being totally present as you're slowly moving along.

Greater understanding of life will come your way when you can appreciate this perspective as well as other ones. Don't limit yourself by always needing to be quick. Choose speed if you need to, but be able to be okay with slowing down as well.

98. Freedom/Structure

I'm freeeee! Okay, now what do I do with myself? I'm tired of these rules, please help me!

It doesn't matter what you have in this world, your mind will surely find a problem with it.

If you have had personal experiences with this, you have noticed that when you have a lot of freedom in your life, then eventually the mind seems to be uneasy and eventually wants some kind of structure. And conversely, if you have tons of structure in your life, your mind wants freedom.

Try to be aware of this in your life. The main thing is to accept what you have at your current moment. If you have structure, then accept it; if you have freedom, then accept that. Of course you can still work toward finding the balance that you want between the two, but don't let it consume your peace.

If you connect to your fundamental nature, you will notice that ultimately you are an infinite being and therefore it is beneficial to have room to expand in every area of your life. It's nice to have some structure, but make sure it's not limiting your expansion.

You can play around with this. Just take a free day and be totally okay with doing whatever comes up for you in the moment. Then take another free day and totally plan it as detailed as possible and stick to that plan.

During this practice, the main thing is to observe how your internal condition is in both scenarios. Notice if outer things can affect your peace, because ultimately that is the only way you can be truly affected.

99. Worshiping

In the beginning, when you are totally lost and need a starting point for anything, it is nice to be guided by someone wiser than you. They can help bring out insights, keep you on course, and get you further than you could have gone on your own.

There comes a time though, that eventually even all wise masters; Buddha, Jesus, Lao Tzu, Muhammad, etc. must be let go of. This is because these entities are all just direction pointers to something that is and has always been beyond themselves.

In fact, if Jesus, Muhammad, or Buddha came back from the dead, they would all be very disappointed that instead of people seeing the truth which was exposed from their authenticity, they have all been made out to be superior beings, unnatural people if you will, that are worshiped without contestation.

It is because of this worshiping nonsense that the truth is hidden from the masses (including you). People continue to seek to find this truth intellectually and not experientially, which is the only possibility. Worshiping creates a dilemma, this is because it says that you believe there is someone that is greater than you, but in actual truth, all is one and one is all. This means neither you nor anyone is greater or less than you. If this is true (needs to be experienced), then how can someone be worshiped? That would make them above you and that's not possible.

100. Complexity

Have you been able to notice yet that everything in this world is so complex that it can blow your mind?

Most people don't take a moment to observe things in much detail, as busy is the mode that they operate in on a daily basis. If this is you, then take your nob on your life speed control and turn it to slow, and start noticing how the most simple things in life, such as a rock, a tree, a plant, a flower, an animal, a bug, a cloud, etc. are the most complex things that you will ever witness.

Go stare at a tree's bark, look at a flower's petals, watch an insect roam, observe a human function, and notice that this stuff cannot be thought up; it's beyond the mind. When looking at these things, notice as much detail as you possibly can, and you will be amazed at what you see, if you actually see it outside of your mind's prison.

ARTWORK

Awareness Elf

Maya

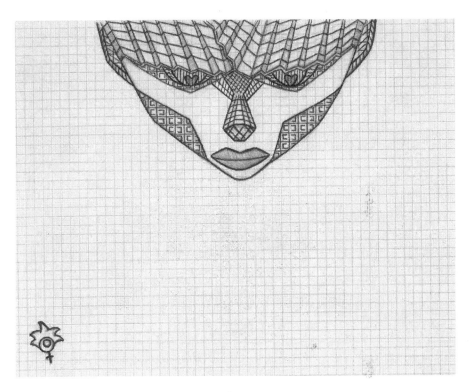

Gem

Wise Man

Life

Infinite Infinity

+

BeHumanNotaZombie.com - Higher Conscious Living

@be human not a zombie - Instagram

Be Human Not a Zombie - YouTube

Pawelwegrzyn.com - Art Portfolio

Thank You

Just wanted to say thank you to all those that helped me along this journey—whether you were the editor, a person that read the book, or just a friend that gave me a kick in the butt to get started—am extremely grateful to you and couldn't have done it without your help.

Made in the USA
Columbia, SC
19 August 2018